Bernard Shaw

BERNARD SHAW

Pygmalion to Many Players

VINCENT WALL

Ann Arbor
The University of Michigan Press

Acknowledgments are made to the following publishers and agents for permission to reprint copyrighted materials:
Atheneum Publishers
    Lawrence Langner, *G.B.S. and the Lunatic.* New York, 1963.
Ernest Benn Ltd.
    Florence Farr, Bernard Shaw, W. B. Yeats: Letters, edited by Clifford Bax. London: Home and VanThal, Ltd., 1946.
The Trustees of the Estate of Mrs. Patrick Campbell
    Mrs. Patrick Campbell, *My Life and Some Letters.* London: Blom, 1922.
David Higham Associates, Ltd.
    C. B. Purdom, *Harley Granville Barker.* London: Barrie & Rockcliff, 1955.
The Society of Authors on behalf of the Bernard Shaw Estate
    Corno Di Bassetto (Bernard Shaw), *London Music in 1888-1889.* London: Constable & Company, Ltd., 1937.
    Bernard Shaw on Music, edited by Eric Bentley. Garden City: Doubleday & Company, Inc., 1955.
    Bernard Shaw: Collected Letters, 1874-1897, edited by Dan H. Laurence. New York: Dodd, Mead & Company, 1965.
    Bernard Shaw, *Complete Plays with Prefaces.* New York: Dodd, Mead & Company, 1962.
    Ellen Terry and Bernard Shaw: A Correspondence, edited by Christopher St. John. New York: G. P. Putnam's Sons, 1931.
Theatre Arts Books
    Bernard Shaw's Letters to Granville Barker, edited by C. B. Purdom. Copyright © 1957, The Public Trustee, Executor of the Estate of George Bernard Shaw. All rights reserved. Reprinted by permission of Theatre Arts Books, New York.

The illustrations listed below are from the following works:
Figs. 3, 7, 8. Reprinted from Archibald Henderson, *George Bernard Shaw: Man of the Century.* New York: Appleton-Century-Crofts, Inc., 1956.
Figs. 2, 4, 11, 13, 14, 16, 17, 18, 20. Reprinted from Archibald Henderson, *Bernard Shaw: Playboy and Prophet,* facing pp. 364, 365, 395, 423, 446, 447, 545, 564. New York and London: D. Appleton and Company, 1932.
Fig. 10. Reprinted from Margaret Shenfield, *Bernard Shaw: A Pictorial Biography,* p. 82. Thames and Hudson, London. © Margaret Shenfield 1962. Photograph from the Enthoven Collection of the Victoria & Albert Museum.
Fig. 22. Reprinted from Margaret Shenfield, *Bernard Shaw: A Pictorial Biography,* p. 83. Thames and Hudson, London. © Margaret Shenfield 1962. Photograph from The Mander & Mitchenson Theatre Collection.

Preface

It was not by accident that three of Bernard Shaw's greatest plays deal with an elderly mentor's attempts to instill wisdom and understanding into a young woman. Caesar finds it to his advantage to teach a savage little Cleopatra how to be a queen; Sir Andrew Undershaft discovers that his daughter Major Barbara is a girl of great spiritual conviction who can be transformed from a Salvation Army lassie into a young woman who can "make war on war"; and in perhaps his most enduring play *Pygmalion* a crotchety, irascible professor of phonetics teaches a cockney flower girl to speak in such a manner that she can become the owner of a flower shop. Shaw was a born educator and the role of teacher to young women appealed to him. Also during the years that he was trying to get his plays before the British public it was to his advantage to find aspiring actresses who could be trained to perform as he wished them to perform. He thus combined his vocation with his avocation, and an enduring record of this exists.

There are many letters to actors as well, of course, but Shaw had a deep psychological and emotional need to write to women. This is especially true of his early days of playwriting when these young ladies needed plays more than did the actor-managers who dominated the London commercial theatre. Shaw was fifty years old when he had his first successes at the Granville Barker's Court Theatre in Sloan Square, and from then on Shaw became a Pygmalion to many players of both sexes.

Bernard Shaw's reputation as a dramatist is so great today that it has obscured the fact that he was deeply in-

volved with almost all of the initial productions of his major
plays in England. The selection of the cast was particularly
important to him since he was writing a new kind of play
that required a particular kind of actor capable of doing
justice to the characters he had created. After the first
reading of the play by Shaw himself, he attended almost
every rehearsal and concerned himself with the minute
details that other dramatists relegated to others. In fact, his
name appears on most of the playbills as "producer" which
at that time in England meant "director" since that word
has only recently begun to be used as it is in this country.

The reason that there is a massive and comprehensive
record of Shaw's work on stage is due primarily to the fact
that at the time Shaw began his work in the theatre, few actors could afford a telephone. Moreover, Shaw was never
the prima donna director who criticized individual actors
before the entire company. Instead, he went home and
wrote out long critiques of what was specifically wrong with
their performance at rehearsal. These he mailed before he
went to bed and the actors received the letters the next
morning. Many players to whom Shaw addressed these
criticisms seemed to realize they were dealing with a
unique dramatist, and they preserved these letters which
now appear in their memoirs. This continued all of Shaw's
life, for he was a compulsive letter writer, and even after actors could afford telephones, he continued to shower them
with written advice of all kinds.

Some of the actresses to whom he wrote letters during
the early years, when he himself was trying to get a hearing
as a playwright, had some professional standing in the
theatre of their day. But all of them were taken on as pupils
by a maestro who felt he was peculiarly qualified to teach
them to perfect themselves in the dramatic arts in order to
properly interpret his plays. Whether they were famous actresses like Ellen Terry and Mrs. Pat Campbell, or whether
they were trying to find success on the stage like Florence
Farr and Janet Achurch, they always were made to feel that
they were the paramount interest in his life at the time. And
they were, for his instruction was really part of an all ab-
sorbing collaboration.

To them he often revealed himself, as if the lonely study from which he wrote were a confessional. Sometimes these letters were the most intimate outpouring of a desperately weary, discouraged, and exhausted man; at other times they were lyrical, ecstatic, and excited accounts of his own creativity. They ranged from hard-as-nails business arrangements to bits of gossip and ephemera of the theatre, literature, the arts, and the larger stage of public life and socialist politics.

These ladies were praised, blamed, threatened, adored, scolded, and cajoled. They were lectured on how to walk, talk, dress, wear their hair, invest their money, and handle all personal relationships. The books they were to read, the music they were to hear, the lectures they were to attend were selected for them. They were even advised as to when and how to divorce their husbands, how to handle their directors and producers, and to what extent they could flirt with their leading men.

When Shaw discovered that Janet Achurch had dyed her brown hair a tawny gold for *Candida* she was ordered immediately to shave her head and buy a brown wig to wear until nature had repaired what Shaw thought was a desecration. Sybil Thorndike was advised, after a reading for the same part, to get herself a husband and four children to prepare herself for the role. Shaw, moreover, expected these commands to be taken seriously. Regretfully, Miss Achurch never paid much attention to Shaw's advice. Miss Thorndike, however, married a fine actor, Lewis Casson, dutifully produced the four children, and was eventually rewarded with a summons to create Shaw's St. Joan. They recognized in one another a dedication that caused Shaw to write in her rehearsal copy: "To Saint Sybil Thorndike from Saint Bernard Shaw."

The available record of the thousands of hours Shaw spent on stage with the players is almost complete. The eight Shaw biographers have dealt with it at least in part; the letters to Granville Barker, to Florence Farr, and Janet Achurch for the early years are all in print; and the letters to Ellen Terry and Mrs. Patrick Campbell have been available for some time. Moreover, the editors of three journals devoted to Shaw criticism have industriously searched for records of Shaw's earliest articles on the art of acting and have reprinted many of them so that all may now be reviewed in proper perspective. It is an imposing record, for few important dramatists had the unique experience of working so closely with the players who interpreted their plays. Shakespeare probably did; Molière certainly did; but Shaw's is the only record that is so extensive that it reveals the author not only in the study but on the stage itself.

Acknowledgments

It is impossible to give proper recognition to the many friends and relatives who helped in the research and writing of *Bernard Shaw: Pygmalion to Many Players*. However, some few both past and present deserve mention.

As an undergraduate at the University of Michigan I was first interested in the plays of Bernard Shaw in the modern drama courses of Professors Oscar James Campbell and Howard Mumford Jones. At Harvard University the poet and scholar Robert Hillyer first revealed to me the importance of the music in the plays. And at the University of Wisconsin, Professor Ethel Thornbury directed my doctoral dissertation on Shaw. More recently many colleagues at Wayne State University read all or part of the manuscript, including Professor Isabelle Graham, Leonard Leone, director of the University Theatre, and his staff. Two of my students, Paula Stone and Stephen MacDonald, were helpful in preparing the manuscript for publication.

I owe a particular debt of gratitude to Vera Scriabine, editor of *The Independent Shavian*, and my many friends among the New York Shavians, Incorporated, who listened to chapters of this book at their monthly meetings. And in particular, I wish to thank Professor Eric Bentley who read the first draft of the manuscript and made many valuable suggestions for a revision, as well as Professor Richard Burgwin of the University of Michigan who also read and annotated the second draft.

I will always be grateful to Ellen Pollack, president of the London Shaw Society, who has created and re-created so many of Shaw's characters on the stage and who allowed me to quote from unpublished Shaw letters in her possession. The librarians at the British Museum were always helpful, as was Lady Nancy Astor who also showed me many Shaw letters in her possession.

Others who helped me in many ways include Alison Tennant Myers, Kenneth and Barbara Davies, my mother, Mrs. Asenathe Ferguson Wall, and my cousin Mrs. Lewis M. Weed whose generosity enabled me to visit England to meet Bernard Shaw and many of his still living friends among the players who brought life to the characters he created.

Contents

I

The Years of Failure

The London Plays and Playhouses in 1890

Today, when almost every important repertory theatre in the Western world presents Shaw plays, and there are frequent revivals of his plays in the commercial theatres, it is necessary to remind ourselves that is was almost twenty years from the time that Shaw began his first attempt at playwriting in 1885 until, in 1904, the Barker-Vedrenne management at the Court Theatre in Sloan Square established Shaw's reputation in England as an important dramatist. Meanwhile, Shaw's plays had become well-known to his reading public. They were successful elsewhere in the theatres of the world, particularly in the United States and Germany. But London was slow to realize that the greatest playwright in the English language since Shakespeare was at work.

An understanding of what Shaw was to attempt to do and why he was to encounter repeated failure to get a hearing in the theatre requires an understanding of the playhouses in England at the turn of the century as well as the players who inhabited them. At that time in central London, which was usually referred to as the West End, there were only twenty-four playhouses. Most of them were on or near Shafstbury Avenue, Charing Cross Road, or the Strand, and were therefore near many of the fashionable restaurants. These playhouses were mainly occupied by what was then known as the actor-managers. Some of these had leases on theatres for as long as twenty years, while others rented different theatres from season to season. Nearly all of them produced plays with prominent parts for themselves and their leading ladies, who were often their wives. Very few of them had anything like a permanent company, although one or two had a nucleus of players who appeared with them year after year.

In addition to the twenty-four theatres in central London, the suburbs had, or were acquiring, a ring of theatres of their own. Many of these were capacious and comfortable houses with very reasonable prices; seats in stalls or balcony were as little as three shillings. To them came touring companies, including many like that of Fred Terry (Ellen Terry's brother) whose romantic costume plays nearly always filled a house for many weeks. It was in these suburban theatres that some of Shaw's own plays were first given in the years before he made a conquest of the West End.

Besides the theatres in London and the suburbs, every major provincial city in England had at least one and sometimes as many as four or five theatres to which the actor-managers brought their London successes (and sometimes their failures!) of the season. It was here that many of them actually recouped losses incurred in London. This was a time when there was no competition from radio, the cinema, or television, and audiences filled all of the theatres outside London's West End to hear the spoken word. But it was the goal of all provincial stock company actors to be asked by some actor-manager to join his London company, and, if he established a reputation and developed a following, to venture into management on his own. It was the age of the great actor rather than the great playwright, although Bernard Shaw, Arthur Wing Pinero, Henry Arthur Jones, and Oscar Wilde were shortly to change all that.

The great years of the actor-managers, according to Lady Frances Donaldson, daughter of the playwright Frederick Lonsdale, were from 1865 to 1914.[1] Lady Donaldson, in her book *The Actor Managers*, lists six who, in her opinion, established the tradition of the great actor-manager who could, if he found the right play, fill houses for most of a season. These were Sir Squire Bancroft, Sir

Henry Irving, Sir George Alexander, Sir Johnston Forbes-Robertson, Sir Herbert Beerbohm Tree, and Sir Gerald du Maurier.

When Shaw was asked to write a preface to *The Theatrical World of 1894* by William Archer, he took the occasion to assess the position of the actor-managers. He named nine who were "practically supreme" as well as one actress-manager, Mrs. John Wood.[2] For some reason he did not include Sir Gerald du Maurier, Cyril Maude, or William Terriss, just as Lady Donaldson does not include one of the most successful actors, Sir Charles Wyndham in her list. The other actor-managers Shaw singles out as important were Sir John Hare, Fred Terry, William Sidney Penley, and John Lawrence Toole. Neither Lady Donaldson nor Shaw mention Wilson Barret, one of the most successful, possibly because he appeared in *The Sign of the Cross* for so many years that he was not involved in many other plays.

By the time Shaw had written ten plays with which he was to challenge the theatre of the nineties, Sir Bancroft and his wife Marie Wilton, who made theatrical history in the sixties by discovering the plays of Tom Robertson, were no longer in active management, and Sir Gerald du Maurier did not go into management until 1910 when he took over Wyndham's Theatre, which became for many years the home of London's most successful light comedies. By this time, however, Shaw was deeply committed to Granville Barker, who continued to produce and direct most of his plays.

Of the four other major actor-managers mentioned by Lady Donaldson, two at least eventually produced a Shaw play. This, however, was after Shaw's first great successes at the Court Theatre. In 1906 Forbes-Robertson began rehearsals in London for an American opening of *Caesar and Cleopatra*, which Shaw had written for him in 1898. In 1913 Shaw and Mrs. Pat Campbell finally compromised on Beerbohm Tree for the role of Henry Higgins in *Pygmalion*.

The remaining two on Lady Donaldson's list, Sir Henry Irving and Sir George Alexander, were each offered one of Shaw's "pleasant plays." Not long after it was written, Shaw read *Candida* to George Alexander, the

handsomest of the actor-managers, who offered to play the
part of Marchbanks if Shaw would rewrite the play making
the "penny poet" (as he called him) blind in order to secure
the sympathy of the audience. Unfortunately, Shaw's
answer to this request is nowhere recorded although it most
assuredly would have been blistering, since this was the second play of Shaw's which Alexander had turned down.
(The other was *The Philanderer,* although it is quite understandable why he did not find the title role in that
"unpleasant" play very attractive. No one ever has; and, of
all the early plays it is the only one seldom performed.) It
might be added that Shaw also failed to seriously interest
Sir Charles Wyndham in *Candida.* Sir Charles wept at the
last act when Shaw read it to him but told him it would be
twenty-five years before the West End would be ready for
such a play.

St. George in Dragon Country:
Henry Irving and Cyril Maude

Although these actor-managers failed to understand Shaw's
Candida, with which a few years later he was to breach the
walls of the nineteenth-century theatre, two others did con-
sider producing the Shaw plays which were offered them.
Sir Henry Irving in 1897 planned to add *The Man of
Destiny* to his repertory of plays and, shortly after, Cyril
Maude actually put another "pleasant" play *You Never
Can Tell* into rehearsal.

Sir Henry Irving at this time was admittedly the most
important actor in the profession by popular estimation.
For almost twenty years the Lyceum Theatre, on which he
had taken a lease in 1878, was the theatre which visiting
celebrities in England wanted to attend. An invitation to his
"after-theatre" suppers in the famous Beef Steak room was
considered an honor even by nobility. And he was the first
actor to receive a knighthood.

The career of Irving is not only typical of the way the
actor-manager handled his little empire, but it is also one of
the greatest success stories in the history of the theatre. A
poor farm boy born of Somersetshire and Cornish stock, he

transformed himself by an incredible effort of will from the stammering, ungainly John Brodribb, into Henry Irving, the epitomy of elegance and refinement on stage and off.

His great success was due in no small part to the fact that Ellen Terry, who joined his company permanently in 1882, also had a tremendous following. The famous Shaw-Terry correspondence had begun in 1892, and was flourishing when, in 1895, Shaw wrote his third "pleasant" play *The Man of Destiny*. Since it was in one act and one set and was in essence a battle of wits between the young Napoleon and a lady over the contents of a dispatch case which she has stolen, Shaw thought Irving could produce it as a "curtain raiser." Miss Terry persuaded him to do so. Up to this time Irving's specialty had been romantic costume plays and Shakespeare.

Shakespeare for Irving, however, meant productions in the nineteenth-century tradition with elaborate sets which required long waits to change, the order of scenes rearranged, and some even omitted. The innovations of William Poel, who produced Shakespeare on an almost bare stage with no scenes omitted and the beauty of the poetry therefore emphasized, were unknown at the Lyceum. Unfortunately, therefore, before negotiations for *The Man of Destiny* were completed, Irving produced *Richard III* in his usual manner, and Shaw, who was now the famous GBS of the *Saturday Review*, wrote a devastating review. He described Irving's performance in an unfortunate phrase as "uncontrolled," which Irving thought meant he had been accused of being intoxicated, although Shaw was later to admit that this only meant that he did not hear some of the great passages in the play that he knew almost as well as Irving. (Probably they were cut.) Shaw was, perhaps, unduly sensitive in feeling that Irving was trying to "buy" favorable notices with the bribe of a possible production. At any rate, the battle was enjoined and even the good services of the kind and generous Ellen Terry, who remained loyal to both men, failed.

Actually Shaw, the critic, had many favorable comments to make on Irving, the actor. It was Irving, the manager, who resolutely refused to consider Ibsen,

Strindberg, or any other of the new dramatists, who was his enemy. If Irving had lent the prestige of his name to productions of any of the new authors, including Shaw, he might have turned the tide in favor of the new drama instead of perpetuating the old.

Rehearsals at the Haymarket

Whether or not Irving ever really intended producing *The Man of Destiny*, at least Cyril Maude put Shaw's third "pleasant" play *You Never Can Tell* into rehearsal at the Haymarket. Cyril Maude had made a great success of the so-called "society comedy" and Shaw felt that this is what he had written. He had gone to the trouble of giving his play a fashionable sea-side setting, with expensive wardrobes for the ladies and a luncheon scene which he felt was necessary for such a play. The vegetarian Shaw had even done some field work for this by attending the famous luncheons hosted by Frank Harris for the *Saturday Review* staff at the Cafe Royal.

You Never Can Tell was written for the most part during the summer of 1895, although it did not go into rehearsal until April 1897. Shaw, himself, was permitted to superintend the rehearsals although he had never performed this function for such an important company. The result was traumatic for all concerned.

To begin with, although Shaw was convinced that he must now write a popular "courtship comedy" for the commercial theatre, his heart was not in it. Time and again while he was writing it he complained to practically everyone with whom he was corresponding that he hated the play and that it was going very slowly. The attempt to pour Shavian wine into this very old bottle was not easy for him, but now that it was written he wanted to see it produced.

Despite Shaw's patient explanation of how he wanted the play acted, the Haymarket Company did not understand him. Winifred Emery (Mrs. Cyril Maude) cast herself for Dolly, but immediately switched to Gloria after hearing Shaw read the play, as he fully intended she should. The part of Dolly then fell to Eva Moore, who hated it. Jack Barnes and Fanny Coleman, two other popular members of the company, threw up their parts after a few rehearsals. "No laughs and no exits," explained Miss Coleman in protest. As usual Shaw confided the nature of his problems to Ellen Terry:

> I sit there and stare at them. I get up and prowl. I sit somewhere else, but always with a dreadful patient and dreadful attention. It is useless to correct more than one speech per person per day; for I find that the result . . . saying the thing as it ought to be said is invariably to paralyze them for five minutes, during which they are not only quite off their part, but utterly incapable of expressing any meaning whatever.[3]

At one point in rehearsing the famous luncheon scene, Shaw felt that he had insulted the entire acting profession by wanting a real table on the rehearsal stage on the grounds that if they didn't have it in rehearsal they couldn't manage the complications of the luncheon scene when they were acting before an audience. Shaw was certainly right here because it is one of the most difficult scenes in dramatic literature to perform properly. In fifteen minutes William the Waiter has to serve an entire three-course lunch to eight people that would take ordinarily two hours. Thus Shaw's meticulous attention to detail, which was to be such an important part of his work as a director, simply could not be understood by a company firmly rooted in nineteenth-century traditions.

Toward the end of April both Shaw and the Haymarket Company could stand the strain no longer and he withdrew the play. If Shaw had persevered (as Ellen Terry wished him to), it would have made a great deal of difference in his attempt to conquer West End audiences; not only that, but Cyril Maude, by playing the part of William the Waiter, would have a more distinguished niche in the history of the English stage than he now does. That the play is eminently actable is attested by the fact that it is the most popular of all Shaw's plays, at least in terms of the number of performances given in professional and amateur acting companies all over the world. S. N. Behrman, himself the greatest writer of social comedy in the American theatre, has called it the best social comedy ever written. It was, however, almost ten years before it would have really successful performances.

St. George Encounters Richard Mansfield and Arnold Daly

Although the neglect of Shaw's plays by the English actor-managers previous to 1904 did not extend to the United States, where Richard Mansfield and Arnold Daly each actually produced some of the plays offered them, there were still many misunderstandings about the nature of the plays.

In the spring of 1894 both Richard Mansfield and his actress-wife Beatrice Cameron Mansfield were in London and saw a performance of *Arms and The Man* at the Avenue Theatre. Mansfield was immediately intrigued with the role of the Swiss Captain Bluntchli, but as the star of his company he disliked the idea of being absent from the stage during the entire second act. Mrs. Mansfield, however, was fascinated with the role of Raina and prevailed upon him to give the play a simple, inexpensive production in New York. That Mrs. Mansfield was right is proved by the fact that it became one of the most memorable performances in her entire career.

Shaw's intimate knowledge of the strength and weakness of his play is evident from a letter of June 9, 1894, suggesting that Mansfield play the part of Sergius rather than Bluntchli. He realized from Florence Farr's Avenue production that, although Bluntchli was an actor-proof part, Sergius was not. He attempted to bait his trap by pointing out that after his entrance in the second act Sergius almost never left the stage, except for one comedy scene between Raina and Bluntchli early in the third act. Whatever else his failings might be, Mansfield was shrewd enough to realize that Bluntchli was the star part and he did not rise to Shaw's bait. Mansfield produced *Arms and The Man*, the first of Shaw's plays to be seen on the American stage, at the Herald Square Theatre, New York City, on Monday, September 17, 1894.

Unfortunately, although a *success d'estime* when Mansfield dedicated his own playhouse, the Garrett Theatre, on April 23, 1895, it was not the financial success which he had hoped it to be. He kept it in his repertory for some time, however, and it made Shaw a considerable amount of money. When Mansfield reported this to Shaw he characteristically replied:

> Of course it (*Arms and The Man*) doesn't draw: whoever supposed it would? It has produced reputation, discussion, advertisement; it has brought me enough money to live for six months, during which I will write two more plays. So take it off in the peaceful conviction that you have treated it very handsomely and that the author is more than satisfied. . . . Judging by the reception of *Arms and The Man*, I cannot doubt that if you were to play *The Philanderer*, you would be lynched at the end of the first act. It exudes brimstone at every pore. . . . I should like very much to see you as Bluntchli. If you will come to London I will even go so far as to sit out *Arms and The Man* to see you.[4]

The result of the relative success of *Arms and The Man* was that Shaw immediately sent Mansfield a copy of *The Philanderer*, in hopes that he would be attracted by the title role. He sent Mansfield his summary of the parts and the kind of casting required for principal roles.

Like all the other actor-managers, Mansfield turned down *The Philanderer* but, after the relative success of *Arms and The Man*, Shaw was able to interest him in *Candida*. In a flattering letter on March 10, 1894, he inquired if Mansfield could play a boy of eighteen; on being told that he could, although some critics might think him too young for the part, he was actually forty at the time, the contract was signed. Mansfield's brother and business manager, Felix, closed the negotiation. Not only that, but Janet Achurch, a relatively unknown actress in the United States, was engaged to play *Candida* in New York (Mrs. Mansfield being ill at the time) for the unbelievable sum of $250 a week. Shaw was nothing if not an excellent press agent. The prospect of having *Candida* produced even at a distance of three thousand miles, and with Janet Achurch as Candida, induced in Shaw a state almost amounting to euphoria.

Letters traversed the Atlantic with every mail boat.
Mansfield was given advice in great detail as to how parts
were to be cast and the play was to be directed. He even
suggested the repertory of plays which were to be included
in the Mansfield season to accompany *Candida.* Quite
naturally they were Ibsen's *Ghosts* and *Hedda Gabbler.* All
this was typical of the way Shaw was to take over the direction of the lives of anyone and everyone with whom he was
associated in the theatre. It must have been one of the major disappointments in his entire life when he received a
letter telling him that Mansfield was canceling the play.
The reason he gave was that he could not possibly make
love on the stage to Janet Achurch, even if he took ether:

> My ideal is something quite different. I detest an aroma of
> stale tobacco and gin. I detest intrigue and slyness and sham
> ambitions. I don't like women who sit on the floor—or kneel
> by your side and have designs on your shirt-bosom—I don't
> like women who comb their tawny locks with their fingers,
> and claw their necks and scratch the air with their chins. . . .
> The stage is for romance and love and truth and honor. To
> make men better and nobler. To cheer them on the
> way—. . . .⁵

This was not the first inkling that Shaw had of his
beloved Janet's weaknesses; but the wonder is that he continued to link his fortunes to her and to her husband after
her return to England. He continued to have faith in
Mansfield in spite of the fact that the actor obviously
wanted a romantic play. Shaw then should not have been
surprised at the way *The Devil's Disciple* was interpreted
by the Mansfields when they brought this first play for
Puritans to the Fifth Avenue Theatre in New York on October 4, 1897.

William Winter, the critic, was enthusiastic over
Mansfield's brilliant acting and with the fusion of high
comedy and melodrama in the trial scene. The *New York
Tribune* review of the première records that:

> After the fall of the curtain at the close of the play, Mr.
> Mansfield was made to appear several times, and he finally
> spoke. He said that it had become the custom for actors
> after they had finished their work in a play to appear to

apologize for the play they had appeared in. . . . He was sure his hearers would agree with him when he said the thought that, though the play was a slight one, it was a very clever one. . . ."[6]

Whether or not Shaw heard of this apology for "a slight but clever work," he was furious because of the romantic interpretation. His fulminations were launched at Mrs. Mansfield whom he somehow felt should have interceded for him. He writes to her on December 10, 1897:

> Thank you for the Philadelphia notices. I informed myself as to the New York production by private reports from trustworthy eye-witnesses, with a result that I very nearly wrote to you about the way in which your business has been spoiled by your monster of a husband. Get divorced, my dear Mrs. Mansfield, get divorced. However, you shall have your revenge. In the next play it is you that shall have the actor-proof part, and he that shall have the uphill work. We shall see then whether he will fascinate New York by carrying hot kettles about the stage. I shall cross the Atlantic someday and play the executioner myself.[7]

Shaw was particularly outraged with some of the business which had been inserted by the Mansfields, including a kiss which again introduced the romantic element in the play which Shaw had been deliberately trying to avoid. "What is to be done with such a man? Can you wonder at my disowning, disclaiming, repudiating? The business of the kiss is Richard's and nobody else's—except of course yours. You could have remonstrated—are there no pokers or carving knives in the house to give emphasis to your protests?"[8]

Having suggested divorce and murder as the only recourse in dealing with such a conceited and egotistical man, Shaw concludes this letter that she will someday have a play all to herself "cramful of irresistible effects."

On the first of January, 1898, he again writes to her, objecting to Mansfield's acting his play as if it were Dickens' *A Tale of Two Cities:*

> I quite understand that the last scene is so arranged that nobody watches Judith, and that the spectacle of Richard Dudgeon making Sidney Carton faces keeps the theatre

palpitatingly indifferent to everything else. And that's just
what I object to: it's all wrong: the audience ought to see
everything—the frightful flying away of the minutes in conflict with the equally frightful deliberation of Burgoyne and
the soldierlike smartness of the executioner: they ought to
long for a delay instead of that silly eagerness to see whether
the hanging will really come off or not and so on. No! I
won't see the other side of it: I'll fight and complain and
extort royalties and be a perfect demon until the parts are *all*
successes."[9]

What all this taught Shaw was the importance of his
being in the theatre at rehearsals if his stage directions were
to be carried out or his lines were to be delivered as written.
Romantic actors would act any play in a romantic manner
no matter what the dialogue and action indicated, particularly if the play were a melodrama.

Perhaps Shaw's realization that it might be some time
before actor-managers would fully understand his meaning
of the play encouraged him to forgive the Mansfields.
Writing to Mrs. Mansfield on March 19, 1898, Shaw wants
to know why she let Mansfield "scorn that little Napoleon
play of mine." Apparently, therefore, Shaw had offered
Mansfield *The Man of Destiny.* He tells her that he is contemplating a play on *Caesar and Cleopatra* for Forbes-
Robertson and Mrs. Patrick Campbell, and asks her if she
fancies those parts for Richard and herself. He also tells her
that he is encouraging the notion in London that Richard is
going "to invade us [with *The Devil's Disciple];* but I have
no hope of his doing so . . . but I have great faith in
Richard's personal fascination in a part which gives him no
opportunity of acting, but allows him to be himself to the
last inch. I know that it is useless to try to make him understand this; but you may have some sure instinct about it."[10]

The Mansfields had been offered six of Shaw's plays
and produced two of them. Shaw certainly should have
been grateful for the fact that he grossed a total of $2,500
for *The Devil's Disciple,* the largest amount of money he
had yet received for any play. It enabled him to marry a
very wealthy woman without being accused of marrying
her for her money.

Arnold Daly, who had begun his career as an office boy for Charles Frohman, had read *Plays Pleasant and Unpleasant* and records that he felt like a prospector when he strikes a big vein of gold. Frohman was at first interested in sponsoring a production of *Candida* for him but later abandoned the idea. The rash young actor with a capital of only $350 finally decided to launch it himself at a trial matinee at the Princess Theater in New York on Tuesday, December 8, 1903. It was an immediate critical success, just as it would be at the Court Theatre in London a year later, and soon found its way into the position of a regular attraction in evening bills. *Candida* not only became a financial success but immediately engendered many critical articles on Shaw in the American literary periodicals. (Several of these were by Archibald Henderson and, on the strength of them, he presented himself to Shaw and became his official biographer.)

Daly followed *Candida* with *The Man of Destiny* and actually several times produced the two plays on the same bill. In addition, Shaw supplied the one act play *How He Lied to Her Husband* (which is really a farcical version of the Candida theme) for him as a curtain-raiser. With these Shaw plays in his repertory, Daly toured the South and the West and eventually New England. He was not satisfied with this success, however, and decided to attempt *John Bull's Other Island* which had just had a great triumphant opening at the Court Theatre in England. It was hardly surprising that New York Yankees were not interested in John Bull's problems in Ireland; there were more Irish in New York than in Dublin at the time but they were not theatregoers, and the play failed miserably.

Now Daly conceived the idea of shocking his audiences into attention with a production of the controversial *Mrs. Warren's Profession*. Although Shaw warned him that this venture was premature and ill-timed, he went ahead with it and stirred up a storm of protest. (It eventually resulted in Shaw's *Man and Superman* being placed on the restricted section of the New York Public Library in September, 1905, which elicited appropriate remarks from Shaw on the subject of censorship in the United States.)

After *Mrs. Warren's Profession* opened at the Garrick
Theatre on October 30, the members of the cast were
arrested on a charge of disorderly conduct and the case was
heard before the court of Special Sessions. On July 6 a decision was handed down acquitting Daly and his manager of
violating the penal code. Justice Olmsted rendered the
following opinions.:

> If virtue does not receive its usual reward in this play, vice at
> least is presented in an odious light and its votaries are
> punished. The attack on social conditions is one which
> might result in effecting some needed reforms. The court
> cannot refrain from suggesting, however, that the reforming
> influence of the play in this regard is minimized by the
> method of the attack.[11]

The damage was done, however, and Daly's career as
the most important actor of Shaw plays in America was at
an end. He had had great success with all four of the
"pleasant" plays but Shaw was never to allow him to perform any of the later plays. This was not wholly because of
the fact that Daly had incurred the ill-favor of press and
public but also, apparently, because Shaw felt that Daly,
too, was not presenting his plays as written.

It must be remembered that Shaw never saw any of
Daly's productions; in fact, he never saw any of his plays in
America. But this did not prevent very cordial relations
existing between Shaw and the Theatre Guild when that
organization began producing his plays and the directors of
the Guild visited Shaw in London. Daly's visits, however,
almost invariably ended in serious misunderstandings.
Lawrence Langner, who has written the history of the
Guild's long relationship with Shaw and who also thought
highly of Daly as an actor and used him frequently, felt it
was primarily because both Daly and Shaw were Irish! Daly
once described to Langner Shaw's directive as to the performing of his plays:

> All that it is necessary for you to do, Arnold, is to say my
> lines so slowly and clearly that the audience can understand
> every word." "What about my acting?" asked Arnold. "As
> long as they can hear my lines, you can act or not as you
> please."[12]

This, of course, was Daly's version of the conversation, but it clearly indicates Shaw thought he was doing too much "acting."

Shaw was always adamant about the players performing his scripts exactly as they were written, including all the business and the stage directions. After writing a play, he worked this out carefully with chessmen on a chessboard representing the actors; these stage movements were then included in the printed play; and the word became the law. He kept close track of what was happening to his plays both from reviews and by word of mouth.

Archibald Henderson, who might have been the tattletale since he was now the official biographer and a frequent visitor in England, records that on one occasion at a dinner party in New York, Daly indignantly denied any tampering with the text:

> I have acted out every one of Mr. Shaw's stage directions to the letter, as far as I am able, with one exception, and that is where Marchbanks goes "trotting" across the stage to the fireplace. I'm too heavy to trot as Shaw meant. Three years ago I could have done it, and now perhaps I might do it three nights in six. But I don't dare risk it.[13]

After his quarrel with Shaw, Daly's career as an important actor-manager was over and, although he had some success in the New York commercial theatre, he began drinking heavily. Langner remembers one performance in a Theatre Guild play when he was so intoxicated that the stage manager, Philip Loeb, had to give him each line from the wings until the pages of the prompt book fell out of his hands and scattered all over the stage. The curtain was rung down on the pretense that Daly was ill. He died in 1928 in his sordid rooming house by accidentally setting fire to himself with a cigarette, apparently in a state of intoxication.

The next day there were headlines on the front pages of all New York newspapers: "Bernard Shaw says of Arnold Daly's death that spontaneous combustion, while rare, sometimes occurs!" Langner was so shocked by this callous remark that he told Shaw the next time he saw him that he couldn't believe he had made such a statement.

No, you are wrong, Lawrence, I did say it, and for this reason: Arnold was no more sentimental about death than I am. He adored publicity, and his death was getting very little of it. Had I made a few pious remarks, they would have gone unnoticed, but I knew that if I made a sensational statement it would make front-page headlines, so I invented the story about spontaneous combustion sometimes occurring, and it had exactly the desired effect. Arnold, had he been alive, would have been delighted to see his name in large headlines in every important newspaper in the English-speaking world.[14]

It could be added that besides perpetuating the Shaw refusal to deliver pious platitudes after a friend's death, the Puritan Shaw would have refused to grieve for anyone whose death was caused by alcoholism and cigarette smoking. Also, he could feel no grief for any performer who did not measure up to his standards of perfection in performance. His rationalization for his macabre joke about Daly's death is an extreme example of similar remarks to and about the players on other occasions.

The trouble Shaw had with both Mansfield and Daly is quite simply that they were actor-managers. This meant they were accustomed to treat authors with the same totalitarian authority that they treated their fellow actors. The lines in a play were simply something they could use as they wished, just as they could alter costumes, stage business, and the position of other actors on the stage.

It is small wonder that after a decade of difficulties with the all-powerful actor-managers, Shaw would turn hopefully to the actresses who had managerial aspirations. When in 1894 he first analyzed the theatrical scene, in his preface to Archer's anthologized reviews, he mentioned one actress-manager, Mrs. John Woods. The only important production he had had in London was Florence Farr's *Arms and the Man* that same year. Shaw was constantly to point out that his plays (like Ibsen's) frequently had better parts for women than men and that was why the actor-managers neglected them, since it was impossible for them to accept second leads. This, however, was only partly the reason that St. George had so many unfortunate encounters in dragon country. Nor was it that his plays were Socialist propaganda; after the first three "unpleasant" plays all such propaganda was skillfully concealed. Also concealed was the "unromantic" attitude of the protagonists of his play for Puritans. Even more unobtrusive was his faith in possibilities of creative evolution which didn't receive major prominence until *Man and Superman*. What really was misunderstood was the kind of acting required to properly interpret the major declamation and the counterpoint of the Shavian music in the plays.

Shaw's Way with a Play

During the last years of his life, long after the struggle for recognition of the Shavian drama had been won, Shaw several times reviewed his early achievements. He also asserted that the new drama of the nineties wasn't all that new:

> The art of all fiction, whether made for the stage, the screen, or the bookshelf, is the art of story-telling. My stock-in-trade is that of Scheherazade and Chaucer no less than of Aristophanes and Shakespeare. I am quite aware that the jigsaw puzzle business, the working out of a plot, is necessary in detective stories, and helpful to playwrights who have talent enough to put their clockwork mice through amusing tricks, and hold their audiences effectively by jury-box suspenses. . . . I could get drama enough out of the economics of slum poverty.[15]

At the same time, Shaw maintained that, instead of taking a step forward technically in the order of the calendar, he had thrown off the influence of the Parisian school and had gone back to Shakespeare, to the Bible, and to Bunyan, Scott, Dickens, Mozart, and Verdi in whom he had been steeped from childhood. Instead of writing carefully in the manner of the well-constructed play, he maintained that he let his plays grow as they came, and hardly ever wrote a page with a knowledge of what the next page would be.

Actually Shaw, consciously or unconsciously in his early plays at least, often wrote a very well-constructed play.

He was willing to work at times through the basic forms
popular in the theatre of his day. Much has been made of
the fact that as a drama critic he ridiculed the artificiali-
ties and elaborate intrigue of Scribe and Sardou. "Sar-
doodledom" he called the carelessly motivated use of stolen
letters, lost wills, purloined jewelry, and overheard conversations. In some of his own plays, however, he does exactly
this, only the blood and thunder is omitted and character
and ideas are substituted for the dependence on mere intrigue.

Henrik Ibsen, the great Norwegian dramatist who was
Shaw's first model, did the same, substituting in the
"discovery" scenes a revelation of the moral guilt of society
for the melodramatic unmasking of villainy. For instance,
in Shaw's first play *Widowers' Houses,* which more than
any other of his plays is patterned on the Ibsen formula,
there are three such revelations. In the second act a young
man learns of his prospective father-in-law's business as a
slum landlord. His engagement is broken off. The next
revelation is that the young man, too, has an income
derived from such substandard housing, since he holds
mortgages on the property. And the final revelation is quite
simply that all society shares in this guilt. The play, being a
Shaw comedy, adds an amusing and initial version of the
battle of the sexes, after which the young couple are reconciled. As Jacques Barzun puts it, "empty out the Shavian
vocabulary and attitudes . . . you will have receptacles in 1,
2, 3, 4 Acts fit for any kind of romantic comedy or thesis
drama you may like."[16]

When Martin Meisel examined Shaw's plays in rela-
tion to earlier nineteenth-century plays he was able to
execute a chart which really fits almost every Shaw play
into a definite category.[17] For instance, *Arms and The Man,*
The Devil's Disciple, and *Captain Brassbound's Conversion*
are all examples of a popular type of play which Meisel calls
"the military romance." Shaw, however, used the
background of war to satirize and ridicule the heroic attitudes taken seriously by previous playwrights. In *Arms
and The Man* the realistic professional soldier shocks the

romantic young lady, in whose bedroom he has taken refuge, by carrying chocolate creams in his holster instead of bullets, since the professional soldier is not interested in being a hero but in surviving the brutal business of war. In *The Devil's Disciple* the Clergyman discovers that he is enjoying his role of leader of the rebellious Americans resisting British tyranny so much that he will leave his pulpit; and the "devil's disciple" will take it over to preach "diablonian ethics." In *Captain Brassbound's Conversion* the popular melodrama of a beleaguered English garrison menaced by savage natives, but rescued by a brave young officer, is turned upside down by having the young commander a traitor seeking revenge for a fancied wrong done his mother; and it is a charming woman whose luminous understanding persuades him to forego his revenge in the second act and who saves him at the subsequent court-martial by a clever presentation of half-truths.

These three "military romances" can illustrate Shaw's pouring of new wine in old bottles. Meisel examines in detail some half a dozen other categories of nineteenth-century drama into which Shaw's plays fall. For instance, the formula of the so-called "courtship comedy" was used by Shaw in *You Never Can Tell, Man and Superman,* and several other plays, but with two new ingredients added. The "courtship" was sometimes really a "battle of the sexes" in which the young lady is the aggressor; and sometimes the play has an unromantic ending that does not lead to matrimony.

Shaw's way with a play did lead to one dramatic form which would be unique and for which he owed no debt to any of his predecessors. This is the discussion play which relies very little on plot. "Talk, talk, talk," says Hypatia in *Misalliance.* Richard Mansfield turned down the part of Marchbanks in *Candida* calling it "talk, talk, talk," and Shaw even proudly proclaimed in one of his last articles on his craft: "Now it is quite true that all of my plays are all talk, just as Raphael's pictures are all paint, Michaelangelo's statues all marble, Beethoven's symphonies all noise." And, of course, Shaw is right. The point is that these artists produced great pictures, statues, and symphonies, and Shaw's talk is the greatest talk to come from a playwright's pen in our day.

The essence of drama is conflict, and Shaw realized that effective conflict in terms of ideas meant that the forces pitted against one another must be equal. As one of his characters, the one-time clergyman Aubrey in *Too True to Be Good* says: "My gift of preaching is not confined to what I believe: I can preach anything, true or false. I am like a violin on which you can play all sorts of music, from jazz to Mozart." Aubrey also elaborates upon this gift which he calls divine:

> It is not limited by my petty personal convictions. It is a gift of lucidity as well as of eloquence. Lucidity is one of the most precious gifts: the gift of the teacher: the gift of explanation. I can explain anything to anybody; and I love doing it. I feel I must do it if only the doctrine is beautiful and subtle and exquisitely put together. I may feel instinctively that it is the rottenest nonsense. Still, if I can get a moving dramatic effect out of it, and preach a really splendid sermon about it, my gift takes possession of me and obliges me to sail in and do it.[18]

Shaw, himself, in the throes of composition must also have felt the same compulsion. This led to the development of style which was more distinctive than that of any other playwright of his day and is due almost entirely to his dialectical approach to his craft. Eric Bentley, one of the most distinguished and discerning Shaw critics of our day, describes this as being simply the "both/and" technique which Shaw developed to replace the "either/or" of other playwrights:

> . . . Shaw is trying to salvage as much as possible both in orthodox and freethinking attitudes to life. Both/And: such is the Shavian inclusiveness. . . . Shaw has tried to balance individualism and collectivism, freedom and authority, diversity and unity, not in the interests of mechanical symmetry, ostentatious broadmindedness, or naive eclecticism, but in an intelligent effort to lay hold of that which is good in each philosophy of life. He has done this as a con-

Edith Evans and Cedric Hardwicke made a great success of Shaw's *The Apple Cart* which was frequently revived at subsequent Malvern festivals, *Left to right, standing*, Sir Granville Bantock, Sir Barry Jackson, Sir Edward Elgar, H. K. Ayliff, Cedric Hardwicke; *sitting*, Edith Evans, Bernard Shaw.

Mr. and Mrs. Mansfield in *Arms and the Man*.

Fig. 2

Ellen Terry as Lady Cicely with her husband James Carew as Captain Brassbound during an American tour with the play.

Fig. 3

Arnold Daly.

Fig. 5

Fig. 4

Florence Farr.

Lillah McCarthy at the time she was creating the leading feminine roles in most of Shaw's plays during the triumphant early years at the Royal Court Theatre.

Fig. 6

Maurice Evans as Jack Tanner in *Man and Superman*.

Fig. 8

ig. 7

Gertrude Lawrence was one of the last Eliza Doolittle's Shaw coached in *Pygmalion*.

Fig. 9

Shaw rehearsing Granville Barker and Lillah McCarthy in *Androcles and the Lion*.
1913 New York Theatre Collection.

Fig. 10

Herbert Beerbohm Tree as the first
Professor Higgins.

Fig. 11

Granville Barker.

Elizabeth Robins, an actress in
Ibsen, whom Shaw greatly admired. She once threatened him
with a revolver during a dressing
room interview and never actually
appeared in a major production of
a Shaw play.

Fig. 13

Fig. 12

Fanny Brough.

Fig. 14

A cartoon of Shaw drawn at the time of the first production of *Fanny's First Play*.

Fig. 15

Arnold Daly's production *Candida* with himself in the part of Marchbanks launched the Shaw boom in New York in 1904. *Left*, Arnold Daly; *center*, Herbert Standing; *right*, Louise Closser.

Robert Loraine as Jack Tanner.

Fig. 16

Sybil Thorndike as St. Joan.

Fig. 17

Shaw wrote *Caesar and Cleopatra* for Sir Johnston Forbes-Robertson who played the part of Caesar for many years.

Fig. 18

Shaw in a publicity picture for a revival of his play *The Apple Cart* at the Malvern Festival.

Fig. 19

Ellen Terry finally played Lady
Cicely Waynflete in *Captain
Brassbound's Conversion* at the
Royal Court Theatre ten years
after Shaw wrote it for her.

Fig. 20

Fig. 21

Fig. 22

Mrs. Pat Campbell as the first Eliza Doolittle in
Pygmalion.

Janet Achurch and her husband
and producer, Charles
Charrington, in Ibsen's *A Doll's
House*.

crete moralist with a feeling for the simplicities, the basic human facts. He has therefore been brought into conflict with the portentous orthodoxies of our time. He has defended socialism against the socialists, liberty against the liberals, science against the scientists, religion against the religionists. Naturally he is accused of being anti-socialist, anti-liberal, anti-scientific, and anti-religious.[19]

When one remembers the dreary thesis dramas of the nineteenth century with the raisonneur appearing front and center to deliver the author's solution, one can appreciate how much superior Shaw's open-end plays really are. A thesis drama with a thesis spelled out means that the play is quickly dated because the thesis is so oversimplified that the more intelligent members of the audience quite justifiably feel that they are intellectually insulted. Shaw is here taking the same position as Bertolt Brecht, who much prefers to have his audiences think things out for themselves. Like Brecht, Shaw wanted his audiences to think passionately rather than to feel passionately. The issues of poverty, war, and crimes against society are so complicated that the solutions offered would be solutions only for a limited length of time.

Shaw learned from Ibsen that the easy solution might produce an "ideal" which very shortly could become a very dangerous ideal, and one which would in turn have to be repudiated. Shaw never really waivered much from the wisdom he put in Ibsen's mouth in *The Quintessence of Ibsenism*—"the ideal is dead, long live the ideal." This is why Shaw's characters in Edwardian costumes can fence verbally with one another with dramatic effectiveness three-quarters of a century after they were created. Perhaps without fully realizing it, he had found within himself a structure and form for his plays. This was the musical forms of opera, symphony, sonata, and oratorio that he had absorbed during his earliest childhood, during his young manhood in London when he was actually trying to write novels, and during those hundreds of hours he was to spend in auditoriums attending concerts which he was to review for London periodicals. This gave a form and structure to his plays that is unique in dramatic literature.

The Art of Acting

With the writing of his first play in 1885, Shaw became interested in the art of acting. The first of three articles which
he wrote in the eighties on the subject was titled
"Qualifications of the Complete Actor" and appeared in
the September issue of *The Dramatic Review*. It was Shaw's
response to letters to the editor from aspiring young actors
asking how they could qualify for success on the stage.[20]
Shaw's article would almost imply that he did not take his
subject seriously, since he indulged in such irony as in-
sisting that the actor learn all modern languages, read the
proceedings of scientific societies and the physiological
journals, learn muscle control and wrestling through gym-
nastic training so as not to leave a single muscle in his body
involuntary.

On September 1, 1886, Shaw took advantage of his
friendship with Annie Besant, editor of *Our Corner*, to
review a lecture-recital given by two American visitors, Mr.
and Mrs. Edmund Russell, on the subject of Delsarté and
his method.[21] Today, in terms of acting, "the method"
refers to Constantin Stanislavski of the Moscow Art
Theatre. During the latter half of the nineteenth century,
however, "the method" meant that of the French singer
and drama coach Delsarté, whose students were taught to
develop all body movements and gestures possible for head,
eyes, lips, torso, arms, chest, legs, and elbows; nothing was
omitted, and all gestures were carefully planned. Shaw
thought himself something of an authority on this subject.
He was, therefore, extremely critical of the Russells,
although he felt that the establishment of a school for acting in London was so important that he encouraged them to
found one.

Shaw's third early statement on the art of acting was
actually a lecture with the enigmatic title "Acting, by One
Who Does Not Believe in It; Or, The Place of the Stage in
the Fool's Paradise of Art.[22]

Some ambiguity arises since Shaw assumes that his
audience is familiar with a book published in 1887 by
William Archer entitled *Masks or Faces*.[23] This book, in

turn, actually was an answer to one by the seventeenth-century French critic Dennis Diderot, which had been translated in 1883 by Walter Herries Pollock as *The Paradox of Acting.* The paradox, according to Diderot, is that to move the audience the actor must himself remain unmoved. Controversies, therefore, arose over how much of an actor's performance is completely predetermined and how much of it is what the actor is feeling while on stage.

What Archer had done was to circulate a carefully phrased questionnaire to some of the most famous performers of his day. This had inspired controversy and not only in theatrical journals. In the May, 1887, issue of *Harper's New Monthly Magazine*, the famous French actor Coquelin contributed an article "Acting and Actors" in which he maintained that there was no such paradox. Everything that an actor did on the stage was sheer technical virtuosity. Sir Henry Irving, on the other hand, in "An Actor's Notes: Number Four" in *19th Century* for June, 1887, affirmed that he, at least, felt everything that he did on the stage; not only his tears but those of his leading lady, Ellen Terry, were real.

In his lecture, Shaw first summarized the opinions of both the "emotionalist" Sir Henry Irving, as well as the complete technician Coquelin. But almost at once he changes his point of view to attack the critics who have created a totaly false impression. The critic, Shaw affirms, "despises the stage as a sham and the actor as a wretched imposter, disguised in the toga of Caesar and spouting the words of Shakespeare." This, Shaw felt, was completely unfair. The actor could, indeed, reply to the critic that although he might be incapable of doing the deeds he was portraying on the stage, could the critics write the scene that he was playing?

Shaw had great respect for a certain kind of actor who is capable of "metaphysical self-realization." Every part he plays will be some new side of his own character and his best part will be that which shows all sides of him and realizes him to us and to himself. When an actor finds such a part "he seizes on it as oxygen seizes on certain metallic

bases. In it he becomes for the first time completely real."
Shaw summarized his main points as follows:

> I will conclude by restating the views upon which I base my
> respect for the actor and the stage, and my despair of the
> critics. 1. That acting, in the common use of the word, is
> self-falsification, forgery and fraud. 2. That the true goal of
> the stage-player is self-realization, expression, and exhibi-
> tion. 3. That the drama can only progress by making higher
> and higher demands on the players' powers of self-
> development and realization. 4. That the critic who rejects
> this view lapses into a vicious contempt for the player and,
> having no valid standard, is compelled to coin convention
> which will not circulate anywhere outside his own circle of
> accomplices. These are the points on which I invite you to
> enlighten me by a frank discussion.[24]

Two of these statements need some explanation. The
first is, that acting is "self-falsification, forgery and fraud."
By this Shaw only meant that what happens on the stage is
an attempt to convince an audience that they are seeing
real people in a real life situation. After the play when the
actor leaves the theatre he naturally becomes another person—namely, himself. The forgery and fraud are over.

The second is the "metaphysical self-realization"
which the great actor embodies in every characterization.
Acting, he advised Henry Irving's grandson, Laurence
". . . must always depend on the success of the pretense
that the character is you, not on the pretense that you are
the character." The actor must not adapt the play to his
own personality, since it then becomes an embodiment of
him rather than the part created by the author. On the
other hand, the actor who pretends that the character is
himself tries to find such aspects of himself as will elucidate
and embody the character, thus adapting his personality to
the play. In this way he realizes the author's purpose to best
advantage.

The Music in the Plays

Shaw himself began telling his critics, early and late, that
they must know opera in order to understand his kind of

playwriting. In one of his last public statements, Shaw summarized his technique:

> Opera taught me to shape my plays into recitatives, arias, duets, trios, ensemble finales, and bravura pieces to display the technical accomplishments of the executants, with the quaint result that all the critics, friendly and hostile, took my plays to be so new, so extraordinary, so revolutionary that the *Times* critic declared they were not plays at all as plays had been defined for all time by Aristotle. The truth was that I was going back atavistically to Aristotle, to the tribune stage, to the circus, to the didactic Mysteries, to the word music of Shakespear, to the forms of my idol Mozart, and to the stage business of the great players whom I had actually seen acting, from Barry Sullivan, Salvini, and Ristori to Coquelin and Chaliapin. I was, and still am, the most old-fashioned playwright outside China and Japan.[25]

This evaluation of three-quarters of a century of playwriting by an author aged ninety-four is at once a criticism and a prose poem. It is also one of his best because it was on one of his favorite topics—himself and his plays. When he compared his plays to operas and oratorios he was really using an expanded metaphor as a poet is entitled to do. And as a poet he meant exactly what he said.

As a writer he thought of himself as a composer, and when he was in the theatre as a director he thought of himself as the conductor of an opera. In an article entitled "*Candida*: The Music of Ideas" in *The Shaw Review*, an ingenious scholar Charles Lloyd Holt has applied this theory to several scenes in that play. The first is between Candida's husband Morell and his curate Lexy Mills. Briefly, the complacent Morell has an aria in which he unctuously tells Lexy that he must find a wife like Candida in order to find happiness. "It is one of the simpler musical forms, a phrase-group or to put it another way, a period with repeated antecedent phrase," he says and amplifies his statement as follows:

> 1) *antecedent phrase*—Ah, my boy, get married: get married to a good woman; and then you'll understand.
>
> 2) *semicadence*—That's a foretaste of what will be best in

the Kingdom of Heaven we are trying to establish on
earth. That will cure you of dawdling.

3) *antecedent phrase*—An honest man feels that he must
pay Heaven for every hour of happiness with a good spell
of hard unselfish work to make others happy.

4) *semicadence*—We have no more right to consume happiness without producing it than to consume wealth
without producing it.

5) *consequent phrase*—Get a wife like my Candida; and
you'll always be in arrear with your repayment.

6) *perfect cadence*—(He pats Lexy affectionately and
moves to leave the room.)[26]

Mr. Holt concludes that this solo by Morell is very
close to a typical musical-phrase pattern. The phrases are
repeated, each one is qualified, and the whole is ended with
a perfect cadence.

Mr. Holt contends that the three principals in this play
(Candida, Morell, and Marchbanks) can be compared to
Faust, Mephisto, and Marguerite in Gounod's opera. In
1891 Shaw claimed to have heard this music drama 90 times
and felt that he had had enough of it. This may be true, says
Mr. Holt, but this did not mean that when he was composing *Candida* in 1894 he did not remember it and have
the essential form so well in mind that he used it constantly
throughout the play, particularly in the last act. These involved, among other things, Candida's three "decisions"
and the three "understandings" attendant on them which
bring the play to a conclusion much as the "seraphic" trio
ends Gounod's *Faust*. Marguerite, like Candida, controls
the melodic development of the final trio. Her three
decisions are translated musically from C-major recitative
into G-major, A-major, and B-major polyphony. With every
key change Marguerite controls the whole. Whether or not
Marguerite "understands" is unimportant, and certainly
Shaw felt that Candida did not understand the secret of the
poet's heart. Like Morell, Faust finally does understand,
although his understanding is acceptance rather than
awareness. It is Mephisto (and therefore Marchbanks), the
realist, who really has the final word. Mr. Holt also feels

that all of this complex musical analogy could be applied to other major plays.

Granville Barker also used the technique of directing Shaw's plays in terms of music. Barker was not far wrong, Shaw tells us in *London Music in 1888-1889*, in describing his plays as Italian opera. The rehearsal at which Barker made this remark was of *The Man of Destiny*, which Vedrenne and Barker had produced at the Royal Court Theatre on June 4, 1907, as a double bill with the dream scene in hell from *Man and Superman* in which Barker played Don Juan. Shaw himself directed the dream scene in hell and no doubt explained to him that the entire play of *Man and Superman* was based on Mozart's *Don Giovanni*.

Theodore Stier, Music Director for the Court Theatre, was later to describe Barker's use of musical terms in his directions:

> There was in Granville Barker's producing a quality of imagination which impelled co-operation from the stage in a way that I have rarely seen equaled, and which to me is very reminiscent of the methods of Nikisch with his orchestra. . . . One of his peculiarities, and one which was curiously effective, was that he would direct rehearsals exactly as he would have conducted an orchestra.
> "I want a tremendous *crescendo* here," he would cry. "A sudden stop. A *firmata*. Now—down to *pianissimo!*"
> Or, again:
> "But, my dear child," he would lament, "you deliver your lines as if you were the trombone, whereas you really are the oboe in this *ensemble*. Remember that, please. The oboe, *not* the trombone.[27]

Barker was also to derive from Shaw the principle of casting characters whose voices were not alike for scenes in which they should play against one another. The four principals should always be soprano, alto, tenor, and bass. This was always the way both men tried to cast the plays for which they were responsible at the Court Theatre.

In directing Shakespeare, Barker was to emphasize the music in the plays, and this, too, was Shaw's idea. You must not only know *Richard III*, he affirmed in reviewing that play, but you must be able to whistle it.

That Shaw's plays have operatic structure is best il-

lustrated by the fact that many of the performers in his
plays who had musical backgrounds immediately
recognized the similarity. For instance, Sybil Thorndyke,
Shaw's original St. Joan, describes her immediate impression after hearing Shaw himself read it. ". . . Shaw knew
every tune of every sentence. I could go through St. Joan
now like an orchestral score. And when I see other people
playing it and they don't do it in the same way, I say, 'you
know, that's not the right intonation.' "[28]

It must be remembered that Dame Sybil's original ambition was to be a concert pianist and to that end she practiced eight hours a day and became something of a child
prodigy. It was only when a form of paralysis prevented her
from realizing this ambition that she turned to the stage. As
a musician she knew the importance of developing voice
control and she went for help to Elsie Fogerty, one of the
great voice coaches of that day. From her she learned the
secret of proper breathing and relaxation:

> She had a wonderful way of focusing the voice and helping
> you to get all the notes. She said, "You must have your three
> octaves." Well, I did have my three octaves until I was over
> 80. And now I have only lost two notes. She had a wonderful
> technical knowledge of the voice. She was often extremely
> tiresome and we could have blown her head off; but she
> knew what she was up to.[29]

Another playwright, actor, and musician Noel Coward,
also realized that he must learn the music in Shaw's plays
rather than just memorize lines. In 1952 he was to appear as
King Magnus in *The Apple Cart* under the direction of
Michael MacOwen. He later told Mr. MacOwen in a television interview that he had learned his entire thirteen
minute speech in the last act in Jamaica before even coming
to London. Mr. Coward believed firmly that the words
must be completely at the actor's command before he goes
into rehearsals. As soon as these began, however, he discovered that playing Bernard Shaw was a completely
different experience for an actor:

> In those long speeches I had to remember my scales,
> because you cannot do a long Shavian speech in a

monotone. You must use your voice, without sounding theatrical, but it must hit this note, that note, that note, this note—you must go up and down without appearing to. But this is not done by just standing on the stage and doing it. When you are reading it and learning it, you've got to decide when you're going to take your voice up, where you're going to lower it, where you're going to do this; and the result has to look as though you were doing it off the cuff.[30]

Mr. Coward gave Michael MacOwen the credit for the insight into the character of King Magnus:

It was you who gave me the clues. I could have played that part off my own bat very effectively, but without you I couldn't have played it true. You told me the one thing that was important; you said, "Keep this in your mind; remember that this is basically a sad man"; and I don't believe that even Bernard Shaw was aware of that. I wish he'd seen it, I love him so. I hope he would have approved of me. But I wouldn't be certain because we played that last act with sentiment, and in the original production there was none.[31]

One thing Shaw would have approved of was the music Coward found in his lines and the structure he was able to give to his big speeches. The reason there is much music in all of Shaw's plays is quite simple: he had been a music critic for seven years. W. H. Auden says with his usual assurance that Shaw was the best music critic who ever lived. Not only was he a great journalist with an easy, provocative style, but he knew music thoroughly. Shaw had lived during infancy, childhood, and young manhood in a house constantly filled with music, both vocal and orchestral.

It is impossible in an age when everybody owns tape recorders, phonographs, and radios to realize the importance of the personal performance of music. The Shaws were naturally a musical family. "All the women could 'pick out tunes' on the piano," says Shaw in the preface to *Immaturity,* "and support them with the chords of the tonic, subdominant and tonic again. Even the Neapolitan sixth was not beyond them."

Shaw's father played the trombone, his eldest uncle, William Gurley, played the ophicleide, a keyed brass bugle, now superceded by the tuba. His Aunt Emily played the violoncello and his Aunt Charlotte the harp and tambourine. It was his mother Lucinda Gurley Shaw, however, who was most responsible for filling the Shaw house at 33 Synge Street, Dublin, with music.

II

The Years
of Preparation

Music in Dublin and London

Shaw's mother Lucinda Elizabeth Gurley was brought up
by a wealthy spinster aunt Ellen Whitcroft, the crippled
sister of Shaw's maternal grandmother. Her upbringing was
rigorous and she was disciplined in all of the conventions
and deportment which would introduce her into the Anglo-
Protestant aristocracy of Ireland. Since she was an attractive
young woman and could be called an heiress, her aunt had
great expectations that she would make a brilliant marriage.

Unfortunately Lucinda Elizabeth rebelled against her
aunt's discipline and chose a husband for herself. This was
George Carr Shaw, also of the Protestant ascendancy, but a
man twelve years her senior with only a small pension.
Lucinda Shaw was, however, a resourceful woman. She was
fond of music and possessed a mezzo-soprano voice often
described as being of a remarkable purity and tone; thus
she decided to study music seriously and for her teacher she
chose George John Vandelour Lee, one of Dublin's most
eccentric music teachers, who lived on the street next to
hers. G. J. Lee, as he was known in Dublin, was a slight,
dark man, crippled in childhood by an accident to his foot;
but a man always described by Shaw as having "mesmeric
vitality and force." He was tremendously ambitious and
must have been something of an opportunist, for he carved

quite a musical career in Dublin not only for himself but for
Mrs. Shaw. In the preface to *London Music in 1888-89*,
which is an anthology of Shaw's musical criticism for *The
Star*, Shaw describes their relationship:

> He trained her voice to such purpose that she became in-
> dispensable to him as an amateur prima donna. For he was a
> most magnetic conductor and an indefatigable organizer of
> concerts, and later on of operas, with such amateur talent,
> vocal and orchestral, as he could discover and train in
> Dublin, which, as far as public professional music was con-
> cerned, was, outside the churches, practically a vacuum.[1]

Shaw says at this time that Lee supplanted his father as
the dominant factor in the household. He appropriated all
the activity and interest of Shaw's mother and they both
became completely absorbed in musical events. Lucinda
Shaw became not only prima donna and chorus leader, but
also musical arranger for Lee's orchestra and band.

Although Lee could not sing himself, Shaw maintains
that his taste in singing was classically perfect. He had gone
to all the best teachers in Dublin to try to find the secret of
Italian *bel canto*.

At the opera he heard an Italian baritone named
Cesare Badiali who, at the age of eighty, had a perfectly
perserved voice and, in Lee's opinion, a perfectly produced
one. Lee was able to watch Badiali perform and discover
exactly what he was doing. He built his theories into a
teaching method which he preached and practiced with
religious fervor. Professor B. F. Rattray in describing Lee's
"method" calls it a "yoga" of Lee's own invention. It was
part of this "yoga" that one could control one's entire body
(not just the larynx) and this Shaw was never to forget.[2] He
was to apply it to the development of his own personality
and he was to dramatize it in his plays. In the dream scene
in Hell of his masterpiece *Man and Superman*, Don Juan
tells Donna Ann that she may be any age she
chooses—seventeen or seventy—and she quite sensibly
settles for twenty-seven. This idea also dominates the whole
last section of *Back to Methuselah* in which the "ancients"
here live as long as they choose and in any way they choose.

This concept was perhaps Lee's most important legacy to Shaw, for it was the cornerstone of his belief in Creative Evolution as a means of creating a superman.

The fame of Lee's method in Dublin soon spread and more and more pupils came to him for instruction. His plans for his career, and for Mrs. Shaw, became more and more ambitious. Using his pupils as a nucleus for a chorus, and the better ones as soloists, his concerts and opera productions became famous throughout Dublin. Obviously more space for rehearsal was needed, and it was decided to unite the Lee and Shaw households at Number One Hatch Street, a four-story house in a more fashionable neighborhood.

Actually the union of households first took place the previous summer at a cottage in Dalkey high up on Torca Hill. From the garden one could see Dublin Bay from Dalkey Island to Howth, and from the hall door there was a view of Killarney Bay with the Wicklow Mountains in the background. Shaw says that Lee bought this cottage and presented it to his mother, though she never had legal claim to it and did not benefit from its sale later on. Shaw was so excited by the beauty of the Dalkey scenery that he describes as the happiest day of his life the moment that his mother told him that they were going to live there.

And it was in this cottage that some of the first rehearsals took place. On October 21, 1905, Shaw sent his biographer Archibald Henderson a photograph taken in 1863, which Henderson called "Lee and his circle at Dalkey County, Dublin in 1863." Shaw describes it as follows:

> This photograph was taken in 1863 by the famous forger Richard Pigott, whose exposure at the Parnell Commission was followed by his suicide in Spain at the moment of his arrest. He was then (in 1863) an apparently harmless and amusing person with a silly-cheerful manner and a single eyeglass, called by his friends "Dick Pigott" or "The Major." The seated figure in the group is George John Vandelour Lee, musical conductor and teacher of singing.[3]

This picture, which has found its way into many of the Shaw biographies, reveals a rather diminutive little man

huddled with folded arms in the exact center of the Pigott
lens and almost smothered by Miss Feeny and Miss Ryan.
Shaw's mother and father are rather austerely standing at
far left and right.

It was not until after Shaw's death that B. C. Rosset, a
seaman, soldier, teacher, and secretary of the Shaw Society
of America, decided to do some research into Shaw's early
years, since he maintained that almost nothing was known
about him for the first thirty-five years of his life. This is not
strictly true but it was enough to motivate Mr. Rosset to go
to Ireland and conduct an exhaustive research in public
records, newspapers, and periodicals from which he might
glean information about Shaw, his family, and friends. He
interviewed all surviving individuals who had some
knowledge of the Shaw family, and he visited churches and
cemeteries to check dates of births and deaths of many of
the principal personae in his story. He even rented a room
in the house at 33 Synge Street (now equipped with indoor
plumbing) and took the daily walks which Shaw took as a
boy. He visited every known building with which Shaw had
any connection and ended up becoming a citizen of the
Republic of Ireland. Greater interest hath no biographer,
and the result was yet another Shaw biography, *Shaw of
Dublin: The Formative Years.*

What motivated Rosset primarily was that Shaw at one
time wanted to set some facts down for posterity and permitted a small volume called *Sixteen Self Sketches* to be
published. One section of this is called "Biographer's
Blunders Corrected." The biographer, who Shaw felt
needed to be corrected, was an American scholar Timothy
Demetrius O'Bolger, whose exhaustive biography of Shaw
was never published. O'Bolger was the son of an Irish police
inspector and Shaw wrote him many letters shortly after
World War I, apparently feeling that there should be a
supplement to the Archibald Henderson biography
published nine years previously.

When the O'Bolger manuscript was finally submitted
to Shaw, he discovered that his new biographer was more
and more insistently inquiring about Shaw's early life and
particularly about the relationship of Shaw's mother and

Lee. Shaw therefore included one of the last letters written to O'Bolger to protest the police inspector technique which he had adopted and which, when the manuscript was submitted to Shaw for his approval, merited his displeasure. At this time, two years before O'Bolger's death, Shaw was apparently apprehensive that the original manuscript, as well as a revised version, would soon fall into the hands of the author's executors. Hence it might subsequently be published under some such title as "The Truth About Bernard Shaw," and he therefore decided to include one letter which revealed his attempts to correct the impression which O'Bolger had gathered that Shaw's mother and Lee were not only business associates with the object of bringing music into a barren land but were actually lovers. The letter begins as follows:

> Dear O'Bolger,
>
> You will certainly be the death of me. As you describe it, my story is one in which the kindly hero, my father, was driven to drink by his wife's infidelity, and finally abandoned to die in the workhouse.
>
> Must I tell you the facts over again? And if I do will they be any more effectual in driving this fictitious item of police news out of your distracted head than my own authentic account?
>
> Just put my mother's singing master and colleague, G. J. Lee, out of your head for a moment. He has not yet appeared on the scene. My father is a middle-aged bachelor, "nobody's enemy but his own." Nobody hates him because nobody fears him.[4]

The letter goes on to point out that after Lee appeared on the scene Shaw's father was perhaps resentful, but came to accept the fact that Lee could provide his family with a larger home at Number One Hatch Street and a better way of life than he could.

Shaw's expressed apprehension that the O'Bolger manuscript might eventually be made known to the public has certainly been justified. Mr. B. C. Rosset for his book consulted both versions of the O'Bolger manuscript in the Harvard Library and subsequently included much of O'Bolger's material in his book. Moreover, after his sojourn

in Ireland, he, too, came to the conclusion that Shaw's
mother and Lee were lovers, and that Shaw was haunted all
his life by the idea that he was really Lee's illegitimate son.
Few of the Shaw scholars who reviewed his book felt that
Rosset proved his case.

Probably the best argument for Shaw's legitimacy is
that all the Shaw children were very fair with blond or red-
dish hair, whereas Lee himself was frequently described as
being "as gypsy-like in appearance as his name." Shaw's
best and lifelong Dublin friend Matthew McNulty
describes Lee as follows:

> He had dark complexion and eyes, hair luxuriant and jet
> black in color, and worn long after the Victorian fashion of
> poets and artists. He had, in addition, a deformed foot. But
> his most striking characteristic was a volubility of language
> which made him easily one of the most tireless (if not
> tiresome) of conversationalists.[5]

The culmination of Lee's musical career in Dublin
came in 1872 with a Dublin Music Festival which included
a chorus led by Mrs. Shaw but with featured soloists
brought from London. The story then takes a turn which, as
Shaw tells it, almost sounds like the libretto for an operetta:

> . . . At a rehearsal the contralto Madame de Meric Lablache,
> took exception to something and refused to sing. Lee
> shrugged his shoulders and asked my mother to carry on,
> which she did to such purpose that Madame Lablache took
> care not to give her another chance.[6]

The result of the success of the Festival was such that
Lee felt that there was but one thing to do; it must be
repeated in London, and as a result he left Ireland for that
city in 1872. Mrs. Shaw, with the Festival applause still
ringing in her ears, very shortly sold the Hatch Street
House, lodged son and husband in a nearby boarding
house, and left Ireland with her two daughters, eventually
to establish herself in London in Victoria Grove off Fulham
Road.

The Religion of the Pianoforte

When Mrs. Shaw left Dublin she sold most of the furniture
at Number One Hatch Street since she needed all available

financial resources for the London adventure. Two important items were not included in the sale of the Hatch Street
effects: one of these was the piano and the other was a great
deal of sheet music and opera scores. In the long evenings
after his work at the office Shaw began teaching himself to
play the piano.

He was motivated primarily by what he called
"musical starvation," which drove him to disregard the
comfort of his fellow lodgers in the boarding house where
he and his father occupied a single large room. Shaw's
method of teaching himself was decidedly unorthodox. He
learned the alphabet of musical notation from a primer and
the keyboard from a diagram. Then, without benefit of any
of the usual finger exercises assigned to the piano student,
he opened his mother's score of the Mozart opera *Don
Giovanni* and went to work. It took him ten minutes, he
tells us, to get his fingers arranged on the chord of D minor
with which the overture commences, but when it sounded
right at last Shaw was able to continue with the rest of the
opera.

At the end of some months Shaw had acquired a
fingering method all his own. Although he was never a vir-
tuoso, Shaw claimed that eventually he could thumb his
way through anything:

> I never mastered the keyboard, but I did a good deal of rum-
> tum accompanying in my first days in London, and even
> once, in a desperate emergency supplied the place of the ab-
> sent half of an orchestra at a performance of *Il Trovatore* at a
> People's Entertainment evening at the Victoria Theatre in
> the Waterloo Road (the Old Vic) and came off without dis-
> aster, and in fact mostly imposed my own *tempi* on the
> amiable and unassertive Italian conductor.[7]

Shaw's hours at the piano were almost his only happy
ones in Dublin. He was becoming increasingly bored with
his job in the land agent's office, which he described as a
treadmill leading nowhere. "Dublin was a desert. London
was the center of art, music and literature."

On arriving in the city of his dreams to join his mother
he was to discover that it was to be as much of a disappointment for him as it had been to her. Both Mrs. Shaw and her

daughter had become estranged from George John (now Vandelour) Lee, who had established himself before their arrival at a fashionable address at Thirteen Park Lane. Mrs. Shaw was shocked to find that Lee not only no longer continued the rigorous and exacting teaching of the method, but had reduced it to a short course of instruction for his wealthy and fashionable West End pupils. She felt that he was a charlatan, and although, as her son puts it, "She dropped him gently," drop him she did.

Shaw's sister Lucy was described by St. John Ervine, who knew her personally, as lazy and ill-tempered. It was because of Lucy's beauty, charm, and talent, however, that she and her brother were invited to at least a few social occasions. There was no doubt of her attraction for men and she attracted some of the oddest. According to St. John Ervine, Oscar Wilde was in love with her as was his brother Willie. It was at Lady Wilde's parties that Shaw met Oscar for the first time and at these occasions Lucy sang for the eccentric Irish expatriates. And now Shaw decided that he, too, would learn to sing properly.

He had, like everyone else in his family, sung as a child, but when his voice changed he fell into the error of trying to gain ends before studying the proper means. He attempted, in properly Shavian fashion, to sing all the parts in the operas and oratorios at the same time:

> In my attempts to reproduce the frenzies of the Count di Luna, the sardonic accents of Gounod's Mephistopheles, the noble charm of Don Giovanni, and the supernatural menace of the Commendatore, not to mention all the women's parts and the tenor parts as well (for all parts, high or low, male or female, had to be sung or shrieked or whistled or growled somehow) I thought of nothing but the dramatic characters; and in attacking them I set my jaws and my glottis as if I had to crack walnuts with them.[8]

Shaw confesses that if he had so continued he would have ruined his voice. Therefore he insisted on being shown the proper way to sing:

> The instructive result was that when, following my mother's direction, I left my jaw completely loose, and my tongue flat

instead of convulsively rolling it up when I operated my diaphragm so as to breathe instead of "blowing"; when I tried to round up my pharynx and soft palate and found it like trying to wag my ears, I found that for the first time in my life I could not produce an audible note. It seemed that I had no voice. But I believed in Lee's plan and knew that my own was wrong. I insisted on being taught how to use my voice as if I had one; and in the end the unused and involuntary pharyngeal muscles became active and voluntary, and I developed an uninteresting baritone voice, of no exceptional range, which I have ever since used for my private satisfaction and exercise without damaging either it or myself in the process.[9]

Shaw is here unusually modest, for there are many testimonies to the fact that he had a very pleasing speaking voice and, although never cherishing ambitions of becoming an actor himself, he always insisted on reading his plays aloud to those interested in them and dramatizing all the parts, both male and female. He had certainly learned a great deal about voice production which he was to impart freely to everyone with whom he was associated in the theatre. Also since he was able to play well enough to function as a rehearsal pianist he was able to be of service to Vandelour Lee.

Lee, now established at Thirteen Park Lane, obtained a position for Shaw as clerk in the music establishment where he purchased the librettos for the operas and concerts he was producing. He also gave Shaw employment in writing press releases for his concerts and, perhaps most importantly of all, made it possible for Shaw to begin his career as music critic by having him ghostwrite reviews in Lee's name for a short-lived periodical called *The Hornet*. These "musical buzzings of a ghost apprentice" began in December, 1876, only six months after Shaw's arrival in London and lasted until September of the following year.

Shaw always liked to say later that it was because of the critical nature of these articles, in particular his championing of Wagner and the "new music," which put *The Hornet* out of business. Certainly these buzzings provided Shaw with some much-needed pocket money. But one thing disturbed him greatly, and this was that, since the articles were supposedly by Lee, the proofs had to be corrected by him. Already Shaw was the perfectionist, but he was as yet in no position to browbeat and terrorize editors and typographers as he was to do in later years.

Another of Lee's projects on which Shaw worked over some period of time was a projected new edition of *The Voice*. This had been originally ghostwritten in Dublin by a doctor of dubious reputation, and by 1882 Shaw was at work on a revision. He had by that time produced five entirely new chapters to which was added another that dealt with the physiology of the organs of sound from the original version. Rosset discovered in the diaries an entry for January 10, 1886, in which Shaw notes that he had "examined various books on music and singing and had prepared a prospectus for V.L."[10]

There is something rather moving about Shaw's description in *London Music* of the decline and fall of the "damaged Svengali" of Thirteen Park Lane. Paying the rent had now become a serious problem and Lee was finally reduced to subletting his rooms for what Shaw calls "merry-making." Lee was still holding out at Park Lane, however, when he dropped dead on November 27, 1886.

The Götterdämmerung that descended over Thirteen Park Lane, however, coincided with a change for the better in the fortunes of both Shaw and his mother. In 1886 Mrs. Shaw was appointed choir director for the North Collegiate School for Girls and in the previous year Shaw had received his first full-time job as a journalist when he accepted a position as art critic on *The World*.

Henry Higgins and Colonel Pickering

One of the really valuable contributions of Rosset's research on Shaw's relationship to Lee was his discovery in the rubble of Shaviana in the British Museum letters and notes from Lee to Shaw proving that they saw a good deal more of one another than Shaw himself has implied in *London Music*. Lee provided Shaw with his first opportunities to learn the rudiments of stage direction and rehearsal. And it was at Thirteen Park Lane that Shaw met several other very important scholars who were professionally interested in just what could be done with the human voice. They were interested in Lee's research for the new edition of *The Voice* because of its application to the study of phonetics.

The young man who first interested Shaw in the study of phonetics and voice production was James Lecky, a civil servant in the Exchequer and Order Department, whom Shaw met through a mutual friend Chichester Bell, a nephew of the inventor of the telephone. Lecky, who always signed himself (phonetically) "jeemz leki," was an accomplished musician and author of the article on "Temperament" (the system of tuning instruments) in the first *Grove's Dictionary of Music and Musicians*, a subject in which he instructed Shaw. It was also Lecky who introduced Shaw to two famous philological scholars, Alexander John Ellis and Henry Sweet, who were to provide Shaw with much of the background for a play he was to write many years later called *Pygmalion*.

James Lecky also was very active in many of the debating societies which then existed in London for the discussion of such men as Darwin, Tindall, Huxley, and Malthus. It was at one of these, the Zetetical, that Shaw made his maiden speech before an audience. This effort was such a failure in his estimation that he decided to improve himself in public speaking. He was embarrassed because of his Irish accent, and Lecky introduced him to a teacher who was to give him a great deal of help in many ways.

This teacher was Richard Deck, an old Alsatian opera singer who was a disciple of Delsarté and had studied acting and voice production with that amazing teacher. Deck was also a disciple of the French socialist, Sully Proudhon. According to Frank Harris, Shaw learned three things from Deck: the first was to abandon plastering his strawberry blonde hair down and to bank it up in the manner familiar to all subsequent caricaturists. Secondly, he taught him how to pronounce French vowels, instead of British dipthongs. Third, Deck was responsible for his training in articulation in which he insisted that his students emphasize consonants for public delivery. Shaw was to repeat this advice to his students: articulate consonants carefully and the vowels will take care of themselves.

James Lecky, too, probably had something to do with the acquisition of the beard, the new hair style, and his vegetarian habit. But the lasting influence on Shaw, and the one that was later to make him feel that he was in every way qualified to be a teacher of voice and diction to the actors in his plays, was the introduction to Henry Sweet and Alexander Ellis.

In the Preface to *Pygmalion* Shaw pays his tribute to Alexander Ellis who, in 1880, was still a London patriarch, with an impressive head always covered by a velvet skullcap. Ellis appears as Colonel Pickering in *Pygmalion*, minus the velvet skullcap, but as a kindly person who helps Eliza Doolittle to become a lady by treating her like a lady. Henry Sweet, whom Shaw admits is at least partly Henry Higgins, was much more rebellious, opinionated, and a great deal like Shaw himself.

What England needed to give the English some respect for their language was an energetic phonetic enthusiast and reformer. Just such a person was Henry Sweet. At Oxford he was a walking repudiation of all its traditions:

> It must have been largely in his own despite that he was squeezed into something called a Readership of phonetics there. The future of phonetics rests probably with his pupils, who all swore by him; but nothing could bring the man himself into any sort of compliance with the university to which he nevertheless clung by divine right in an intensely Oxonian way.[11]

Shaw goes on to say that Higgins is not an exact portrait of Sweet, to whom the adventure with Eliza Doolittle would have been impossible. He admits, however, that there are touches of Sweet in the play:

> With Higgins physique and temperament Sweet might have set the Thames on fire. As it was, he impressed professionally all Europe to an extent that made his comparative personal obscurity and the failure of Oxford to do justice to his eminence, a puzzle to foreign specialists in his subject.[12]

It was from Sweet that Shaw acquired the habit of listening intently to all conversations within earshot. He also prided himself, as did Sweet, on being able to establish the exact part of the United Kingdom from which the speakers came, as well as parts of the Empire where they might even have lived or visited. An example of this in *Pygmalion* occurs when Higgins, identified at this point in the play only as the notetaker, establishes the origins of both the bystander and Eliza, the flower girl:

> *The Bystander.* He aint a tec. He's a blooming busybody: thats what he is. I tell you, look at his boots.
> *The Note Taker* (turning on him genially). And how are all your people down at Selsey?
> *The Bystander* (suspiciously). Who told you my people come from Selsey?
> *The Notetaker.* Never you mind. They did. (To the girl) How do you come to be up so far east? You were born in Lisson Grove.
> *The Flower Girl* (appalled). Oh, what harm is there in my leaving Lisson Grove? It wasnt fit for a pig to live in; and I had to pay four-and-six a week. (In tears) Oh, boo—hoo—ooo—
> *The Notetaker.* Live where you like; but stop that noise.[13]

The notetaker is subsequently able to tell that Colonel Pickering, whom he also has just met, has a background that includes Cheltenham, Harrow, Cambridge, and India. They now introduce themselves and retire to Higgins' laboratory in Wimpole Street. It was from Sweet also that Shaw developed his own peculiar way of occasionally giving his Cockney characters speeches transcribed phonetically. One of Eliza's first speeches is an example:

> *The Flower Girl.* Ow, eez ye-ooa san, is e? Wal, fewd dan y' de-ooty bawmz a mather should, eed now bettern to spawl a pore gel's lahrzn than ran awy athaht pyin. Will ye-oo py me f'them? (Here, with apologies, this desperate attempt to represent her dialect without a phonetic alphabet must be abandoned as unintelligible outside London.)[14]

Shaw began transcribing cockney dialect in his novels almost as soon as he met Henry Sweet. The first major character in the plays who speaks in dialect is Candida's father Burgess. A great deal has been written about this scene-stealing character who represents Shaw's ability to delineate through speech what Burgess really is. Shaw was even interested in re-working Burgess's language long after the play had been written and performed. The standard edition of *Candida* contains much more detailed phonetic transcription than did the play as it was originally published.

St. John Ervine, who also rather fancied himself something of an authority on cockney dialect, had a good many arguments with Shaw over the character of Burgess. Ervine found him "unconvincing" and felt that it was incredible that this "vulgar ignorant guzzling man" (as Shaw describes him in a stage direction), should be the parent of such a gracious and refined woman as Candida. There is something to be said for this, for unless Candida had spent some time in boarding schools with teachers as brilliant as Henry Higgins it seems impossible that she could speak as she does in the play. Ervine calls Burgess "a low form of cockney," which Shaw vehemently denied and provided a detailed description of his background:

> Burgess was born in 1840 in Oxfordshire, or possibly of Oxo-
> nian parents in Hackney; which then had turnpike gates and
> pigs running about the road, miles and atmospheres from
> the sound of Bowbells. To this day, and certainly to the date
> of Candida, even Shoreditch is less completely cockneyfied
> than Charing X: cockneyism, being smarty always went west
> and not north or east. Burgess, with his emotional rhetorical
> L's, is studied closely from a well known and long deceased
> Oxford character. He does not utter a sound of modern
> cockney; and the difficulty I have at rehearsal . . . is that
> Burgess will try cockney.[15]

The next Shaw character who speaks almost entirely in phonetic transcription is the cockney Drinkwater in *Captain Brassbound's Conversion*. Here again Shaw creates a comic effect, contrasting the vulgarity of the character's speech with the shrewdness of his wit. John A. Mills in *Drama Survey* has analyzed Drinkwater's speech habits in considerable detail. On every possible occasion Drinkwater

speaks in a rich tone of sententiousness which contrasts with
the grossly inept nature of his speech:

> . . . with unflagging singleness of purpose, Drinkwater
> borrows fine words and phrases which his capricious
> cockney tongue can only render in the most absurdly dis-
> torted fashion. Whether solemnly murmuring the cliches of
> Christian comfort or sobbing out the formulas of pulp fiction
> bathos, he consistently arouses comic pleasure by the con-
> trast of these tinsel terms with the hard realities of his
> cockney articulation.[16]

In this play Shaw also makes some attempt to distinguish between the speech of the English characters and
the American captain. He apologizes also for the fact that
he makes no attempt to transcribe phonetically the speech
of Lady Cicely and Lord Howard. Actually Shaw feels that
he owes Drinkwater some apology for implying that his
vowel pronunciations are unfashionable:

> They are very far from being so. As far as my social
> experience goes (and I have kept very mixed company) there
> is no class in English society in which a good deal of
> Drinkwater pronunciation does not pass unchallenged save
> by the expert phonetician.[17]

He concludes his notes on this play by admitting that
he has made only the most perfunctory effort to represent
the dialect of the missionary. There is no literary notation,
Shaw feels, "for the grave music of good Scotch." In other
words, Shaw's use of phonetic transcription for his comic
characters is purely for the sake of comic effect. In the
speech of Eliza Doolittle's father, Shaw uses the same comic
contrast in his extremely colorful vocabulary derived from
the cockney dialect in which they are uttered.

Also in both Eliza Doolittle and her father there is
comic contrast when they are undergoing their transfor-
mations after their introduction to a better society. One of
the most amusing scenes in all Shavian literature is that in
which Eliza is shown off in Higgins' mother's drawing
room. After her set speech about the weather she is so
carried away by the occasion that she rattles on describing
the most intimate details of her cockney life, in particular

the ladling of gin down her dying grandmother's throat, but using now the West End pronunciation which she has been taught. Shaw, as always, was deeply resentful of the fact that many men and women had to be constantly humiliated by their speech patterns when they appeared in public. This is why he has his phonetics professor take on the difficult task of correcting his student's speech. By so doing Shaw is able to make an important statement on the place of speech in British society and on the deplorable lack of suitable training in the phonetics of the English language. Henry Higgins, as well as Shaw, is actually distressed by Eliza's language:

> A woman who utters such depressing and disgusting sounds has no right to be anywhere—no right to live. Remember that you are a human being with a soul and the divine gift of articulate speech: that your native language is the language of Shakespeare and Milton and The Bible; and don't sit there crooning like a bilious pigeon.[18]

Perhaps the really revolutionary change in terms of linguistics which was suggested to Shaw by Henry Sweet was the creation of a new phonetic alphabet. Mrs. Higgins, in the third act of *Pygmalion*, refers to her son's habit of writing postcards in his patent shorthand, by which she meant Sweet's *Current Shorthand* which was published by the Clarendon Press. Shaw tried to learn it several times but eventually gave up and used the Pitman system, since this was the one his secretary was able to transcribe. (Shaw, when in the throes of composition always felt he could not write fast enough; therefore he followed Sweet's example of using shorthand to "glean his teeming brain"). Sweet's *Current Shorthand*, although it was phonetically accurate, since Shaw claimed it could express every sound in the language, vowels as well as consonants, ended up almost becoming a private language which could only be understood by very few disciples. But Shaw took to heart Sweet's true objective which was to provide "a full, accurate, legible script for our noble but ill-dressed language."

Many years after Sweet's death Shaw was still convinced that the English alphabet was utterly ridiculous and therefore English spelling was ridiculous. This was why English children (and actors) could not be successfully taught to speak because they also could not be taught to spell.

That Shaw was deeply concerned about the difficulty of human communication is illustrated by the fact that at his death he left all of his considerable fortune for the foundation of an entirely new English alphabet to be composed of something like forty letters. It would be like Henry Sweet's, a one-sound-one-letter alphabet of twenty-four new consonants and sixteen new vowels. These letters also would be represented by utterly new symbols so that no one could possibly mistake the new spelling for the old. Shaw felt that what was really needed was an orthographic revolution.

Shaw's ashes had scarcely been strewn about his rose garden at Ayot St. Lawrence when trouble arose. He had anticipated this, since he provided that in case his will was set aside by the courts his money would be divided equally between the British Museum, the Dublin National Gallery, and the Royal Academy of Dramatic Art. Only about 28,000 pounds of the estate were allotted by British law to Shaw's project, however. Some of the money was assigned as a prize for devising the new alphabet, which was won by Kingsley Reed, who put forty-eight characters into his alphabet, among them sixteen vowels. Also *Androcles and The Lion* has been published in this new alphabet as directed by Shaw.

Many agreed with the judge who "broke" the alphabet trust, including Shaw's long-time friend the American born Lady Astor. Many others, including Barbara Smoker, at that time President of the Shaw Society of England, were indignant. Miss Smoker, who has made a lifelong study of Shaw as a phonetics expert, not only thought that Shaw was completely serious but that the result that Shaw anticipated might have been forthcoming. Shaw always felt that international wars were largely the result of the members of the human race being unable to communicate with one another.

Shaw anticipated the vagaries of British law by setting up his alternate bequests, and the one to the Royal Academy of Dramatic Art would not have been altogether displeasing to him. He had advocated such an institution long before it was founded at his Majesty's Theatre in 1904 by Sir Beerbohm Tree, who ten years later was to create the role of Henry Higgins.

III

Love and Lessons

Madge Brailsford: A Fantasy

Fortified by his knowledge of the work of Henry Sweet and Alexander Ellis in their phonetics laboratories, by research in the British Museum on George John Lee's *Voice*, and his knowledge of Lee's famous "method," Shaw was now ready to look for pupils whom he might instruct in the art of acting. Since he began his literary career as a novelist, it was quite to be expected that his first pupil was really a character in his third novel *Love Among the Artists*, written in 1882. Here we find Shaw introducing a musician and teacher of phonetics whom Stanley Weintraub, editor of *The Shaw Review*, compares to the author who created him. "Shaw's passionate belief in his own talents and his bitterness at being thwarted are reflected in the neglect of the novel's hero, a British Beethoven,"[1] says Mr. Weintraub. He calls this composer, Owen Jack, not only an early Shavian man of destiny but a Pygmalion-figure anticipating Eliza Doolittle's mentor, Henry Higgins. In one of the parallel plots of the novel Jack undertakes the training of an actress, Madge Brailsford, in voice, elocution, and poise.

Owen Jack is something more than just a Shavian *alter ego* who actually, as a musician, achieves the success Shaw was hoping to achieve as a novelist. He is also a most entertaining character in himself as well as a relentlessly demanding voice coach. Poor Madge has almost as hard a time with Owen Jack as Eliza Doolittle, a quarter of a cen-

49

tury later, will have with Henry Higgins. The further she progressed the less she could satisfy him (Owen Jack). His ear was far more acute than hers; and he demanded from her beauties of tone of which she had no conception and refinements of utterance which she could not distinguish. He repeated sounds which he declared were as distinct as day from night, and raged at her because she could hear no difference between them. Henry Higgins will be making much the same demands on Eliza, sometimes reducing her to tears and tantrums.

A second bit of advice Owen Jack gives his pupil is on the occasion of a disastrous encounter with one of the many actor-managers of the day. This actor, a pen portrait, according to some, of Barry Sullivan, behaved in the fashion of many of these egocentric artists and subordinated not only Madge's part but all others to his own position on stage, always front and center. Jack suggests ironically that Madge must herself become an actress-manager so that she can herself dictate her own terms to the rest of the company.

A third aspect of the relationship of pupil and teacher that anticipates *Pygmalion* is the teacher's reaction to his pupil's declaration of love. Owen Jack explains to Madge that he expresses his passion in his music and that "my art is enough for me, more than I have time and energy for occasionally." To her question, "And so your heart is dead?" he answers, "No: it is marriage that kills the heart and keeps it dead. Better starve the heart than overfeed it. Better still to feed it only on fine food, like music."[2] Here Shaw was using what he will later call the most deadly of all human conflicts—the struggle between the artist-philosopher to escape the clutches of the wife-mother in order to pursue his life's work. In this novel, Owen Jack emerges victorious, as does Marchbanks with Candida, whom the poet leaves to her domesticity so that he can create his vision of a better world.

It is true that some later Shavian protagonists in the plays (like Jack Tanner in *Man and Superman*) are caught in the tender trap. But with *Love Among the Artists* the genuine artist-philosopher escapes to devote himself to his art to the exclusion of romantic attachments. Elsewhere in the novel he contrasts the real artists with second-rate artists who are not inspired and who do not have a "passion for beauty" as well as the ability to create it.

How much of Shaw himself is in this novel really is not so important as the picture he gives us of a gaslit London of horse-drawn cabs and stuffy Victorian respectability. Mr. Weintraub calls *Love Among the Artists* a "conversation-novel" and it is true that the plots and subplots are not as interesting as the characters presented. It is, however, the only one of Shaw's novels that could properly be called a novel of manners, and as such it can stand on its own merits. The world of art, artists, and pseudoartists is well drawn. Particularly good is the contrast we get of Owen Jack, the composer-genius, as a Beethovenish bull, nonchalantly crashing about the Victorian drawing rooms.

One well-realized scene in the novel is Owen Jack's rehearsal of one of his "advanced music" compositions which has been rather reluctantly accepted for performance by a very conservative club of musicians. It is, however, a triumph for the "new music" and, one might add, the "new morality." This challenge to the old order was always to be one of Shaw's criteria of greatness.

Most interesting of all, however, is Owen Jack's demands on the promising actress Madge Brailsford. He is more successful than Shaw himself was to be when he became his own Pygmalion to flesh and blood actresses.

Actually the first of these was shortly to come into his life, according to Shaw's friend and biographer St. John Ervine. It is recorded in Shaw's unpublished diaries that on August 7, 1884, he began the instruction and training of a Miss Consuelo. She had called at the Shaw house wishing to be taught a part in a burlesque at the Gaiety Theatre before the following Monday. Shaw's mother being out of town, Shaw himself volunteered to help her. He gave her lessons on the ninth and tenth, presumably using the method of instruction which his mother used for her singing pupils. Shaw went to the first performance of the burlesque and wrote Miss Consuelo a note about it. She sent him a box of silk handkerchiefs which he returned, and this is the last we hear of her. There is a hiatus of some four or five years before Shaw, now the well-known music critic GBS and Fabian platform performer, finds actresses worthy of his coaching.

Florence Farr: "My One Best and Truest Love"

On February 24, 1888, Shaw wrote to Alma Murray, an actress who had had some success as Beatrice in Shelley's *The Cenci* for the Shelley Society and was shortly to appear as Mildred in Browning's *A Blot on the Scutcheon* for the Browning Society. He had the year before seen Miss Murray in a play called *Christina* by Percy Lynwood and Mark Ambient, which he thought particularly bad:

> I wish I could write you a real play myself; but unfortunately I have not the faculty. I once wrote two acts of a splendid play, and read them to an eminent dramatic critic. He laughed the first to scorn, and went asleep in the middle of the second; so I made him a present of the MS (to his intense indignation) and set to work to destroy the society that makes bad plays possible. What a career you will have when that work is completed![3]

The play, of course, was *Widowers' Houses,* then known as *Rheingold,* and the drama critic was William Archer who was, in a sense, Shaw's collaborator at the time since he had provided the scenario for it. The dialogue was all Shaw's and some three years later he was to regain sufficient confidence in his ability as a playwright to complete the third act of the play which established him as a dramatist to be reckoned with in the history of English literature. The actress who created the part of Blanche Sartorius in *Widowers' Houses* was not Alma Murray, however, but Florence Farr, a young woman with whom he was to be closely associated for the next few years, as was another young Irish *emigré* recently arrived in London, William Butler Yeats.

No biography exists of Florence Farr, who achieved some small success at the turn of the century as an actress, playwright, novelist, and poet. Since she figures prominently in the lives of both Shaw and Yeats, a great deal is known about her. She was not only on intimate terms with both men but both singled her out to perform in their plays and both wrote plays for her. Both also took it upon themselves to instruct her in exactly how they wished their plays to be performed, and this record is not only a comment on the theatre world of their day but also on the dramaturgy of these two important men of letters.

Both of these men met her at about the same time and the same place. The year was 1888 and the place, the converted coach house in Hammersmith of William Morris, the artisan, poet, and medievalist who was a friend of all three. Although Yeats has been called the last of the Romantics, and Shaw called himself the first of the "Unromantics," and although one eventually became a great dramatic poet and the other a great lyric poet, their background was very similar, and they had many attitudes in common. The essential difference in the two men was in the field of economics. Shaw, as a Fabian Socialist, impressed Yeats not at all, for, except for some lip service to the beauties of the speech of the Irish peasantry, he was politically an aristocrat. The lectures on socialism in the William Morris carriage house, delivered by "the barbarian of the barricades" (as he was later to call Shaw), fell on deaf ears. And one remembers that Yeats said he once dreamed of Shaw as a "smiling sewing machine."

One personality trait that Shaw and Yeats had in common is responsible for most of what is known about Florence Farr. Both had what almost amounted to an obsession for correspondence—mostly with attractive young women. That is why Florence Farr at the time of her death possessed a large amount of correspondence from both of them. The circumstances surrounding the preservation and eventual publication of this correspondence is in itself something that almost savors of romantic fiction. In 1912, the eventual editor of the correspondence, Clifford Bax, was living with his first wife in a Wiltshire manorhouse, and Florence Farr was invited to stay with them. "At the time of our meeting," says Bax, "she must have been about fifty, but she was still beautiful and no one who saw her could forget her starry eyes. She was, in fact, one of the four or

five genuinely poetic women whom I have known. And
during her stay with us she talked a good deal about oc-
cultism, one of her deepest interests, and it must have been
on account of those talks that I came to possess the letters."[4]
Before she left England to become a teacher in a Vedantist
seminary on the island of Ceylon, Miss Farr sent Clifford
Bax a locked black box, with a request that it not be opened
until he should hear of her death. She died on April 29,
1917. The letters contained in the box were finally cleared
for publication many years later in 1946, and are very
revealing of the formative years of both poets. Unfortunately none of Miss Farr's letters to them survive, although she
is mentioned some fifty times in the Yeats' letters and
almost as many times in the Shaw correspondence.

Although Florence Farr was temperamentally much
closer to Yeats, she did share one enthusiasm with Shaw
that led to an almost immediate intimacy with him. That
was the plays of Henrik Ibsen, which at this time Shaw was
busily explaining to a nation that had been horribly shocked
by the great Norwegian. He distilled the best of this
criticism into *The Quintessence of Ibsenism* which, dis-
counting some Shavian distortions, was by far the best account of the playwright in the English language at the time.
Since Shaw was going to write plays in which he was planning to bring new life and new ideas to the English theatre,
he was going to look for Ibsen actresses who could be
trained to act in Shaw plays. He thought he had found such
an actress in Miss Farr and immediately set about
educating her for this important task and, incidentally, fell
deeply in love with her.

In Shaw's first letter on January 5, 1891, he calls her
"my other self—no, not my other self, but my very self."
But the fact that Shaw was both lover and teacher is clearly
indicated by the fact that after the above declaration he immediately begins to scold her for failing to comprehend the
lessons in voice production that he had learned from
listening to his mother coach her pupils:

> There is nothing that drives me to such utter despair as
> when I make some blundering and unsuccessful attempt to
> make you see some technical point that my mother can

teach to any idiot in a few lessons; and you shrink as if I were disparaging your artistic gifts. You do not know the importance of some of these tricks as regards health, economy of physical force, self-containedness and the like.[5]

This very well indicates Shaw's belief that the great artist must have devotion to his craft, as opposed to the practices of the many actor-managers of Shaw's day who merely looked for vehicles in which they could run through the tricks that pleased their audiences. Shaw was shortly to begin writing plays that called for a rhetorical and operatic style of acting, and he realized that he must find and train artists who could successfully interpret the great arias, duets, and quartets that he was to write for them.

Perhaps Shaw's greatest contribution to Miss Farr's career at this time was persuading her that the Ibsen part best suited to her was that of Rebecca West in *Rosmersholm* rather than Ellida in *The Lady From The Sea*. According to one critic they even played *Rosmersholm* together privately in Bloomsbury. In any event, when Miss Farr appeared in the play when it was publicly produced she achieved success, at least in the opinion of the avant-garde critics. She studied hard, although never hard enough to please a relentless taskmaster. After the first private readings (which were apparently attended by William Archer, Shaw's friend, one-time collaborator, drama critic, and at that time Ibsen's translator) Shaw has this to say about another facet of her career:

When Archer says you want grip, he misses the problem in your case. You will never proceed by way of grip, but by sustained beauty of touch. But touch on what? On a conception of your part so complete that it accounts for every moment of Rebecca's time while she is on stage. That is what demands such frightful labour of invention—such years of time. At present there are innumerable gaps and holes in your conception: it is whilst you are passing through these that your "grip" is lost. Yet these gaps with you are not absolutely blanks. They are rather places where you fail in intensity of realization and certainty of execution. You fade rather than vanish. And at all times you yourself are there, never quite insignificant. I am always reassured when I see you: even when I am not satisfied, I am not disappointed:

there is no air of failure in anything you do. And I am not impatient—only frightfully afraid that you will get impatient with me and my criticisms.[6]

In spite of all these reservations, by 1891 Florence Farr appeared on Shaw's honors list of Ibsen actresses. In the "Appendix to the Quintessence of Ibsenism," which appeared only in the first edition of 1891, she is listed, along with Janet Achurch, Elizabeth Robins, and Marion Lee as being among the first to recognize the importance of the Norwegian dramatist. All of these actresses were in touch with advanced thought and came to the stage from outside the theatrical class. Shaw has a great deal to say here about the professional rivalry of the two schools of actresses. Miss Farr's school maintained, according to him, that the professionals were "ignoramuses," while the old school retorts that Miss Farr was only an amateur. Both schools, however, are amateur, says Shaw, when the word means "unpracticed executant":

> The old technique breaks down in the new theatre; for though in theory it is a general technique of application making the artist so plastic that he can mold himself to any shape designed by the dramatist, in practice is but a stock of tones and attitudes out of which the appropriate selection and combination, a certain limited number of conventional stage figures can be made up. It is no more possible to get an Ibsen character out of it than to contrive a Greek costume out of an English wardrobe; and some of the attempts already made have been so grotesque, that at present when one of the more specific Ibsenian parts has to be filled it is actually safer to entrust it to a novice than a competent experienced actress.[7]

This would indicate that Shaw was whole-heartedly on the side of the new school whose members were products of the movement for the higher education of women. But at the same time Miss Farr needed a great deal of coaching, since she was not born into the theatre and had much to learn in terms of voice production, which Shaw set about teaching her.

Shortly after their work on *Rosmersholm* was finished, Shaw began his own career as a playwright. This took place when J. T. Grein, after a sensational opening of his

Independent Theatre with Ibsen's *Ghosts*, decided to produce *Widowers' Houses*, and Florence Farr had progressed sufficiently in her studies that her coach (and lover) cast her in the part of the feminine lead, Blanche Sartorius.

Miss Farr's appearance in this play led to several other engagements. All during the year, however, when the overworked Shaw was writing this play, there were quarrels—real lovers' quarrels and reconciliations. But he still persevered with her education; he even pays her an unprecedented compliment on August 8, 1891:

> Prithee persevere with thy speaking: I found with unspeakable delight last time that you were beginning to do it quite beautifully. There is much more to be done, of course, much ill usage in store for you, but success is now certain. You have reached the stage of the IDIOTICALLY BEAUTIFUL. There remain the stages of the INTELLIGENTLY BEAUTIFUL and finally the POWERFULLY BEAUTIFUL: and until you have attained the last you will never be able to compel me to recognize the substance of that soul of which I was shown a brief image by Nature for her own purposes.[8]

Shaw seems here to be anticipating what he was later to dramatize as the life force which would be developed in later plays. This is certainly a revelation of the feeling that at one time operated powerfully within him. Almost at no other time in these early years do we find Shaw revealed as a sincerely passionate lover. Not only was he a lover, but he was capable of being a jealous lover. "Now listen to me," he tells her on January 28, 1892, "When you tell me that I best know what I am, I assent, not with humility, but with towering head striking against every star and raising great bumps on them; so that astronomers reel amazed from their telescopes." Shaw already had the utmost confidence in his own genius. He tells Miss Farr that he is the noblest creature that she has met and that her other lovers were mere monkeys:

> Some of them thought you a pretty female ape: others thought you a goddess: the first asked you to play with them; the second asked to be allowed to worship you: you

could not say NO to either. Then came I, the man, and made
you my woman on your stopping me as I wandered lonely
through the forest and asking me to look earnestly at you.
For many years had I wandered alone, sufficient to myself: I
will, at a word, wander on again alone. But what will you
do? Return to the monkeys? It is not possible. Self-sufficient
must you also become or else find no less a man than I to be
your mate.[9]

Shaw was probably being unreasonable. He was a busy
man, not only with his work on *Widowers' Houses* but with
many Fabian meetings and lectures as well as his concert
reviews. He was also still seeing Jenny Patterson; and if he
objected to the monkeys in Miss Farr's life, it was quite
reasonable that she should object to Jenny Patterson. Mrs.
Patterson was a well-to-do widow, older than Shaw and actually a friend and pupil of his mother. On Shaw's twenty-
ninth birthday she "aroused his curiosity" as he tells his
biographer, Archibald Henderson, and they were intimate
for the next few years, although never to the exclusion of
other interests on Shaw's part. When Shaw became interested in Florence Farr she sensed that this was a serious
relationship, as indeed it was. On one occasion she even in-
vaded Miss Farr's flat when Shaw was visiting her and
become violently abusive to both of them. Shaw was finally
forced to send Miss Farr from the room to prevent Jenny
from attacking her physically, and it was several hours
before Shaw could persuade her to leave the premises. This
was almost the end of that relationship. Shaw was later to
dramatize the scene in the first act of *The Philanderer*,
although that play was not produced until many years later.

The Princess and the Actress

At this time in Shaw's life his romantic attachments with actresses became somewhat complicated because Janet
Achurch and her husband Charles Charrington had
returned from an Austrialian tour. Almost immediately they
became involved in London productions, and Shaw was to
become one of their chief advisers and consultants. From
now on his fortunes (and misfortunes) as a playwright were

to be closely bound up with them, and so were those of Miss Farr.

Janet Achurch first appeared on the English stage in 1883 at the age of nineteen. After the usual career in pantomime and melodrama at the Adelphi, as well as some Shakespeare with Frank Benson on tour, she finally found her play. This was Ibsen's *A Doll's House* in which she appeared on June 7, 1889, at the Novelty Theatre. This was not the first production of that play, since there had been a previous adaptation by Henry Arthur Jones. Also Eleanor Marx Aveling, Karl Marx's daughter, had not only translated the play, but had appeared in it in an amateur performance, with Shaw playing the part of Krogstad, one of his few known performances on the stage. This was Shaw's introduction to Ibsen, and he later claimed that he didn't understand a word of his part, although he was subsequently to become Ibsen's foremost champion in England.

Janet Achurch and her husband had now produced it in a professional style and it created great critical excitement; the avant-garde spectators cheered and the old guard booed, and Miss Achurch was launched on a career as an Ibsen actress for the rest of her life. She and her producer-husband, and often leading-man, however, were always in dire financial straits and always borrowing money. Indeed the production of *A Doll's House* was typical of Janet Achurch's conniving. She had gone to Henry Irving to ask help in putting on the comedy *Clever Alice* at the Novelty Theatre on which the Charringtons had obtained a lease. Irving responded generously with an unexpectedly large donation of one hundred pounds; instead of *Clever Alice*, however, the Charringtons produced *A Doll's House*. Irving made no known comment on this misappropriation of his funds. He did go to see the play and was depressed by the performance. Since the play became something of a *succès de scandale*, the run was extended from seven performances to twenty-four. In spite of this the Charringtons lost seventy pounds and subsequently had to leave London for a two years' tour of Australia. On their return, they wanted to do a popular play and chose *Adrienne*

Lecouvreur by Eugene Scribe and Ernest Legouve in an adaptation by Henry Herman. It was presented at the Royalty Theatre in April, 1893, for only a few performances.

Although considered by some to be the best of almost four hundred plays Scribe worked on (mostly with collaborators), it is a classic example of all that Shaw disliked about the French well-made play of intrigue. The intrigue here is particularly complicated and involved the rivalry for the love of Count Maurice de Saxe of a popular Comédie française actress (the Adriennce Lecouvreur of the title) with a French Princess.

The play is full of the usual complications of mistaken identity, lost jewelry, and intercepted letters of assignation. Originally written in 1849, *Adrienne Lecouvreur* served as a vehicle for Sarah Bernhardt. Later in translation it was played by Mme Ristori, Mme Modjeska, and Miss Helen Faucit. Now, in spite of her devotion to Ibsen and the new drama, Miss Achurch chose it for her return to the London scene, and also chose Florence Farr to appear opposite her as the Princess. There is probably no real significance to this; Shaw's relationship with Miss Farr was over, and his intimate relationship with the Charringtons had not yet progressed very far; *Candida* was still unwritten.

The performance at the Royalty Theatre that Shaw attended brought forth a letter to Miss Farr blasting both the play and her performance. If it gave her any satisfaction, he tells Miss Farr that Janet was "transcendantly bad," but he continues with a devastating critique of her own performance. "In the first scene," he tells her, "you are insufferable. You wave your arms about like a fairy in a transformation scene, obviously *pretending* to make an impossible toilet. You must invent something real to do, or else simply put on the patch intently, carefully, resolutely (as becomes a poisoner potential) and then study yourself thoughtfully in the glass, like an artist in the art of dress. If you decide at any time to do nothing, shut your mouth and compose yourself, and *do* nothing."[10]

Besides disapproving of the stage business of Miss Farr in creating this role, he accuses her of mumbling her lines.

(This, of course, was unforgivable after the hours of training Shaw had given her in diction). He tells her that she should balance her torso on her pelvis, and her head on her torso, so they stand erect by their own weight. This would enable her by a very slight movement of her head to draw back with dignity when she is confronted by Adrienne in the play.

With regard to the confrontation scene also, Shaw gives Miss Farr some sound advice. He tells her that she should carefully insult her opponent by not attending to her and turning her face to the audience. She is not to look at her adversary as she senses that she is approaching, but when she has finished her last line then she should turn and face her for the first time. He concludes by telling her that the sooner the play disappears the better for the reputation of the Charringtons.

It is typical of Miss Farr that she took no offense at this rather brutal criticism, and a year later, in 1894, the pupil was able to render considerable service to the master when she produced his first "pleasant" play *Arms and the Man.*

In the spring of that year, Miss A. E. F. Horniman, a wealthy patroness of the arts, volunteered to finance a season for Miss Farr at the Avenue Theatre (later the Playhouse). Miss Farr asked Shaw for permission to revive *Widowers' Houses* but he offered her instead his first "pleasant" play *Arms and the Man.* This was preceded by Yeats' one-act play *The Land of Heart's Desire* in which Miss Farr also appeared.

Arms and the Man opened to rather mixed notices, including that of the "unscrupulously honest" William Archer, as H. G. Wells once called him. As the drama critic of *The World,* Archer even refused to review productions of Ibsen's plays which he himself had translated into English and also was reluctant to give favorable reviews to friends and fellow socialists. In this play he felt that Shaw was wrong in mixing what he called a "realistic comedy" of Balkan life with a "military fantasy." The audience, however, seemed to enjoy it. An incident occurred on the opening night of the play that gave rise to one of the Shaw legends. When he was giving a speech at the final curtain

he was greeted by a solitary "boo!" to which Shaw replied:
"My dear fellow, I quite agree with you; but what are we
two against so many?" The editors of *The Theatrical Companion to the Plays of Shaw* record that the audience
"broke into spontaneous cheers."[11]

The fact remains, however, that the audiences of the
mid-1890s were not ready for Shaw (or Yeats). Shaw felt
that part of the reason for the extent of Miss Horniman's
losses (some four thousand pounds) was bad management
and lack of publicity. Shaw once estimated that if the total
audience attending the fifty-one performances had all
appeared in the first two weeks and the expenses of the
production then terminated it would have been a financial
success.

But it did give Shaw the only run in London of any of
his first ten plays. It also gave him his second opportunity to
function as producer and director—two roles he was
anxious to assume. But it was almost the end of his close
personal relationship with Miss Farr. In October of 1896
there was an angry exchange of letters, the exact nature of
which is obscure since Miss Farr's letters to Shaw have not
been preserved. But there is a definite valedictory pro-
nouncement from the playwright; and this time he really
meant it. On October 12, 1896, she is a lost wretch, "as for
me I can wait no longer for you: onward must I go for the
evening approaches. To all your flower maidens I have
given more than you gave me, and offered more than any of
you would take. My road is the high road; and your bypaths
and shortcuts only lead backward."[12] Two days later he
pens a real valediction. He warns all mankind to beware of
women "with large eyes and crescent eyebrows and a smile
and a love of miracles and moonshees." He declares that
she is utterly selfish and an irreclaimable idiot and one
whom destiny had mocked with great opportunities never
realized. "I renounce spiritual intercourse with you. I con-
demn you, during all our future meetings and bicycle rides,
to talk instead of listening. I may possibly, being the greater
intelligence, learn something from you. From me you can
learn nothing."[13]

The Passionate Puritan to His Love

Shaw did not lose confidence in the Charringtons even after the ill-advised production of *Adrienne Lecouvreur*. Janet was also forgiven for her part in the *Candida* debacle in New York with Richard Mansfield. After all, it was Mansfield's failure to understand the play that was responsible for his decision to withdraw it, rather than the fact that he did not relish playing opposite a leading lady who reeked of nicotine and liquor. If Mansfield had known, as did Shaw by this time, that she was also a narcotics addict, he would have blamed Shaw even more for saddling him with a relatively obscure English actress whose salary had to be paid even though she was not performing.

It is almost typical of Shaw's belief in himself as a teacher that he felt he could make over both the Charringtons in his own image. He could rescue Janet from the bottle and the needle and at the same time improve her acting.

She was to be the recipient of almost as painstaking and rigorous training as that which had been offered to Florence Farr. In one letter, for instance, Shaw tells Charrington:

> You must let me schoolmaster Janet in my unsympathetic manner however it may wring your heart, because you are a very unfit person to educate her. You are rather like Hedda Gabler in respect of your having discovered so much of what was shoved down your throat as virtually would be a fraud, that you idealize the repudiation of the seven deadly virtues. Now in art this does not do. You must plod away diligently in the situation of life to which your vocation has called you, making the work always as good as you can . . . in fact, you must conquer the domain of virtue before you make the devil a present of it; and it is as the family chaplain that I am going to be useful to Janet who has many shocking little vices that must be cast out with prayer and fasting.[14]

Immediately after the Charrington's return from Australia and New Zealand, Janet received a long critique on both of their performances in their revival of *A Doll's House* at the Avenue on April 19, 1892. He first offers an

explanation for Clement Scott's "onslaught" on the production in *The Telegraph*. In her absence Scott had been
"grievously abused" by Shaw, William Archer, and Arthur
Bingham Walkley for the position he had taken as self-
appointed spokesman for the anti-Ibsenites.

Shaw then begins his own onslaught. Charles was now
playing Helmer instead of Dr. Rank as he had in the
original production in 1888. This was all wrong, although
Shaw felt that this was not his fault because the part of
Helmer was not in his nature. Charrington's strong point
was that he could play with conviction; what was wanted
for Helmer was complacency without conviction, and
Charrington was playing with conviction without complacency.

Shaw's "onslaught" continues with Janet's new Nora:

> As to Nora, the difficulty about her is that she had no ar-
> tistic conscience. During her travels her voice has become
> much more powerful—quite Hyde Parkian in its pedal
> notes, in fact; but she has scandalously neglected to cul-
> tivate the beautiful, reposeful, quietly expressive, infinite-
> ly inflectionable normal voice, neither raised nor lowered,
> which is the great charm of a fine speaker. She explodes into
> fortissimos during which she forgets all about the
> tone—forgets the one constant tender care which never
> deserts the great artist. . . . I refuse to tolerate any Nora who
> tightens her lower lip like an india rubber band, and then
> speaks by main force, exulting in the strength of her youth. I
> am not to be propitiated by an increase in tragic power,
> however striking. Anybody can be tragic if they are born so;
> but that every stroke shall be beautiful as well as powerful,
> beautiful to the eye and ear; that is what I call art.[15]

Shaw goes on to drive home his point when he gets to a
criticism of the second act of the play:

> The tarantella began at the pitch which it should only
> have touched for the 1/10000000th of a second at the end. I
> believe you deliberately seized the scene round the waist
> and ran away with it until it was spinning fast enough to run
> away with you. You were excited—a most unpardonable
> thing in an artist. . . .
>   . . . . I admit that your comprehension of the part is

extraordinary, and that you make it live in the most glowing, magnetic way. But Nora may be Nora, and even Norissima—I am not denying that you are Norissima—and yet she may cruelly starve and baffle the artistic appetite—the appetite for beauty and grace.[16]

Shaw concludes this letter by preparing an agenda of future Ibsen plays for the Charringtons. They must do *Rosmersholm* since Rosmer would be a great part for Charles; and they must do *Hedda Gabler without* Charles as Lovborg. Shaw felt that Lovborg had no intention of using Hedda's pistol when she gave it to him, and that Charles's "conviction" would make the audience feel he would. This interpretation of *Hedda Gabler* is debatable, but Shaw had just sent the Charringtons his *Quintessence of Ibsenism*, which explained his position.

In *The Quintessence* Shaw had produced a serviceable guide to the already published plays of Ibsen. And in explaining Ibsen, he had succeeded in explaining what the Shavian theatre was and would be. As a Fabian he had continued to think of a rationalistic socialism of the kind taught by John Stewart Mill. To this, from time to time, he had added the Marxian ideas of the inevitable class war, although the Fabians still looked for an evolution to socialism by way of the ballot-box rather than the barricades. In the face of too great complacency, however, Shaw would sometimes threaten his readers (and listeners) with possible violence. This, however, was later, after he had begun to despair of man as he was and to develop his dream of a superman. Back in 1891 he was to add, somewhat illogically, the romantic individualism of Ibsen, together with odds and ends of Ruskin, Schopenhauer, and Shelley to his Fabianism. In terms of the plays themselves he was to stress the sickly conscience of the middle class who had substituted slavish devotion to "duty" and outworn "ideals" for a clear-eyed realism which would not tolerate excuses and compromises. Slavish devotion to ideals, especially the mistaken idealism of Gregers Werle in *The Wild Duck*, was particularly dangerous. And the new Shavian dramaturgy was to hold it up to ridicule.

The Quintessence was sent to the Charringtons as

homework to catch them up on what had been going on during their absence. And a great deal had been going on. There had been the production of *Ghosts* by the Independent Theatre that had aroused the anger of Clement Scott. London had also seen the productions of Miss Farr's *Rosmersholm*, Miss Fraser's *A Doll's House*, and, most important of all, the *Hedda Gabler* of Elizabeth Robins and Marion Lea. These young ladies were American actresses who were to be very prominent in the avant-garde English Theatre, particularly in the production of Ibsen.

Elizabeth Robins had traveled in Norway and had become aroused by the power of Ibsen's plays of social realism. On arriving in England she had played Martha Bernick on July 17, 1889, in *Pillars of Society* and Mrs. Linden on January, 1891, in *A Doll's House*, and had aroused the interest of William Archer, now Ibsen's official translator. Archer had never shared Shaw's enthusiasm for Janet Achurch or Florence Farr and thus it was that Miss Robins obtained the acting rights to many of the later Ibsen plays with the result that the Charringtons would have to look elsewhere for plays. Shaw would, of course, oblige and thus *Candida* became Janet's play with the result that has been described.

A letter written to Charrington in March, 1895, indicates how closely he felt his destiny was tied up with the Charringtons. He was to write a new kind of play and they were to be "schoolmastered" in the art of performing in it:

> . . . Nature gave Janet a success half ready made, and enabled her to do things with impunity for which I should, so to speak, have been pelted from the stage and sacked next morning. I want a revival of the art of beautiful acting; and I know it to be impossible without tremendous practice and constant aiming at beauty of execution, not through a mechanical study of poses and pronunciations (though every actor should be a plastic and phonetic expert), but through a cultivation of delicate feeling, and absolute renunciation of all the coarser elements of popularity. And I must lay my plays out for that. You have no idea, I believe, of the limitations under which I write, the constant search for the right sort of distinction, whether of style, or thought, or

humor, or vulgarity—how very nicely I have to ascertain the truth in order that I may find the true error with such precision as to make it appear that it was the first thing that came into the head of the character into whose mouth I put it. . . . I will let emotion and passion have all the play I can in my characters. But you must recollect that there is distinction even in emotion and passion; and that the finer kinds will not run through the wellworn channels of speech. They make new intellectual speech channels; and for some time these will necessarily appear so strange and artificial that it will be supposed that they are incapable of conveying emotion. They said for many years, remember, that Wagner's endless melody was nothing but discord.[17]

In London the lives of the Charringtons took on a pattern which was also that of many others who had dreams of conquering the West End. They would lease a theatre, put on a play which would lose money; then they would take some of their past successes (like *A Doll's House* in which Charrington was now playing Dr. Rank) to provincial cities, such as Manchester, where Janet's grandparents had been actors, and here make some money which they would gamble on another attempt to play in London.

Meanwhile the family chaplain, the Puritan Shaw, counsels Janet again and again to follow the religious life, to read the gospel of St. John and the lives of the saints. They will do more for her, he tells Janet, than morphia pretends to do. She must watch and pray and fast and be "humbly proud." Then all things would be added unto her.

Little by little Shaw became more and more disillusioned. Although the Charringtons produced *Candida* on tour he would not allow them to bring it into London. Janet's vices were more and more apparent, and there seemed little chance that she would change her way of life. She even signed some of her letters to him "bad lot," an indication that that was what she thought herself to be and what she had every intention of continuing to be.

IV

From Sloane Square to the West End

Little Eyolf
At the Independent Theatre

When Charles Charrington became director of the Independent Theatre, one of their projects was a production of Ibsen's *Little Eyolf* which was as yet unproduced in London. William Archer was the translator, Janet Achurch was to play the feminine lead, Elizabeth Robins held the English rights to the play, Charles Charrington was to direct, William Heineman (Ibsen's publisher) was being solicited for additional funds to supplement the £400 which had already been raised; the letters flew back and forth and Shaw seemed always to be at the eye of the hurricane. It was a very revealing controversy not only of Shaw but of many of the actresses with whom he was involved. The trouble with the Independent Theatre's *Little Eyolf* in 1896 began with the casting of the play which contained three important female roles. Three of the actresses with whom Shaw had been involved—Janet Achurch, Mrs. Pat Campbell, and Elizabeth Robins—were contenders for the parts.

While Janet Achurch had been playing 150 performances of *A Doll's House* in Australia, New Zealand, India, and Egypt, Elizabeth Robins had all but replaced her in London as the most important Ibsen actress. Miss Robins' greatest triumph came after the Charrington's return, when, in 1893, she and Herbert Waring produced the William Archer and Edmund Gosse translation of *The Master Builder,* in which they played Hilda Wangel and Halvard Solness. They had played a fortnight of matinees at the Trafalgar Square Theatre beginning Monday, February 20, 1893, and had then had an unprecedented run of afternoon and evening performances, from March 6 to March 30, at the Vaudeville. An Ibsen performance in the evening, according to Miriam Alice Franc in *Ibsen in England,* was almost unheard of. Not only that, but Miss Robins followed up this success with what almost amounted to an Ibsen Festival at the Opera Comique at the end of May and beginning of June, with revivals of *Hedda Gabbler, Rosmersholm,* and even the fourth act of *Brand* on a double bill with *The Master Builder.*

Shaw, although still GBS, the music critic for *The Star,* naturally wanted to interview this newcomer. He did so on February 4, 1893, and at the end of the· interview, according to Shaw's diary note she "got rather alarmed . . . and swore she would shoot me if I said anything she did not approve of."[1]

The interview was not published, but a tantalizingly brief account of it is contained in a letter to Miss Robins written on the following day. He includes what might be excerpts from his notes at the interview: "sensational headings ad lib . . . lustrous eyes . . . Ibsen's masterpiece . . . if you do I will shoot you . . . the revolver is there. . . ."[2] He tells her that, although he had interviewed many beautiful women before, never had he had such success. He will, for her sake, sacrifice it all—or at least reserve it for his autobiography. He then gives her ten rules on how to conduct herself at an interview, and concludes by asking to be invited to a rehearsal.

Shaw had seen *The Master Builder* twice, once at the opening with William Archer, after which he sent Miss Robins a note in which he attests "the perfect success of the play," although Herbert Waring as Solness was not quite able to carry through the second act. He does not have the "mystery" and fascination for it, but he has never acted better:

I shall say nothing about Hilda, as she is an ungovernable person off the stage and would take anything I could say in bad part. Her conduct presents only one extenuating circumstance—she sent me a ticket as a sort of atonement for having treated me very badly.[3]

After seeing it for a second time at a matinee on March 3, Shaw wrote again:

Your own playing was much better—surer, intenser, triumphantly convinced and convincing. I confess to a complete renewal of any admiration for your great artistic control. It was really a noble and beautiful performance. At the same time I hasten to relieve you from any sense of being disarmed against your will by assuring you, in our personal, non-artistic and non-critical relations, of my unmitigated defiance, and resentment of the wounds you have dealt to my justifiable vanity.[4]

The next letter was written after seeing Miss Robins's *Hedda Gabbler* at the Opera Comique on June 5, 1893. He had escorted May Morris to the evening performance, but apparently he sent her home in one hansom cab and started the journey home with Miss Robins in another. This time he was not threatened with a revolver but was, he says, "seized and flung out of the vehicle into the mud, with wheels flying over me this way and that and horses dancing and stumbling on my countenance." He admits that he could not help being in love with her at this moment "in a poetic and not in the least ignoble way." But Miss Robins must have sensed this "by a sort of devilish divination" and reacted accordingly.

Considering Shaw's humiliation at this time, it is proof of a forgiving nature that he should three years later be trying to get Miss Robins for the part of Asta Allmers in *Little Eyolf*. He was by this time not only a drama critic but also a stockholder in the Independent Theatre. His efforts here, however, were complicated by the fact that her chief rival was a Miss Rhoda Halkett, a protege of Ibsen's publisher William Heineman, who was also a potential investor. Shaw had been telling Mr. Heineman that it would help the sales of the printed plays to have *Little Eyolf* seen in the theatre, but he could not see the very curvaceous

Miss Halkett as the self-effacing Asta Allmers. Miss Robins was not by character self-effacing, as Shaw very well knew, but she was, he felt, a sufficiently good actress to play the part. She was a veteran Ibsen actress and besides, thanks to Archer's interest in her, she controlled the acting rights! Shaw eventually had his way and prevailed over the Charringtons as well as Mr. Heineman, and Miss Robins was cast as Asta.

Janet Achurch was quite naturally the choice for the feminine lead of Rita Allmers, and Courtenay Thorpe, who had been playing Torvald Helmer in A Doll's House for the Charringtons, was cast as Alfred Allmers. Little Eyolf was produced at the Avenue Theatre for matinees beginning November 23, 1896, and was immediately something of a success.

Shaw, as GBS of the Saturday Review, begins his review of the play by analyzing it. He maintains that Little Eyolf is an extraordinarily powerful play although perhaps inferior to some of the earlier masterpieces. It is the story of a marriage—an "ideal marriage" from the suburban point of view; but, of course, an absolute horror from the Ibsen point of view. A young gentleman, a student and teacher, falls in love with a beautiful and wealthy young woman. Since she has a great deal of money she is able to release him from the drudgery of teaching; this is just where the usual English play of suburban life concludes with a happy ending, but where the Ibsen play begins. Ibsen's play concerns the increasing jealousy of the wife of her husband's use of his new found freedom. His refuge from his wife's devouring passion is in his peacefully affectionate relations with his half sister, the writing of a book on "human responsibility," and the education of their crippled son. Now there appears on the scene what Shaw calls "Ibsen's divine messenger." This is a strange old woman called the Ratwife who appears to ask if there are any little gnawing things there of which she can rid the house. There are, of course, many of them, including the crippled child who follows her to the harbor where he is drowned. The part of the Ratwife was played by—of all people—Mrs. Pat Campbell.

Mrs. Campbell's appearance in the cast is not too surprising, however, when one realizes that the Ratwife is a beautiful cameo part—one of Ibsen's greatest. She is on the stage for but one scene and the stage is all hers. After that, Mrs. Pat Cat, as Shaw was then calling her, could retire to her dressing room for champagne.

Shaw says in this review that he has seen Mrs. Campbell play the Ratwife on two previous occasions, once quite enchantingly, once most disappointingly. On the first occasion she played supernaturally and beautifully:

> The first notes of her voice came as from the spheres into all that suburban prose: she played to the child with a witchery that might have drawn him not only into the sea, but into her very bosom. Nothing jarred except her obedience to Ibsen's stage direction in saying "Down where all the rats are" harshly, instead of getting the effect in harmony with her own inspired reading, by the most magical tenderness.[5]

The next time she played the part, to Shaw's unspeakable fury she amused herself by playing like any melodramatic old woman, "a profanation for which . . . never will I forgive her."

Miss Robins's production of this play was a tremendous success, and Shaw was naturally delighted that Janet Achurch had finally achieved a part worthy of her talents as the jealous wife. The parts of the Ratwife and the sister Asta act themselves. Rita Allmers, on the other hand, Shaw declares to be one of the heaviest parts ever written by Ibsen, but Miss Achurch was more than equal to the occasion:

> Her power seemed to grow with its own expenditure. The terrible outburst at the end of the first act did not leave a scrape on her voice (which appears to have the compass of a military band) and threw her into victorious action in that tearing second act instead of wrecking her. She played with all her old originality and success, and with more than her old authority over her audience.[6]

This was the old Janet, and in this play Shaw greatly approves of her volcanic approach. She was the incarnation of impetuous, ungovernable strength.

Her interpretation of Rita Allmers did strange things apparently for Miss Robins's interpretation of the sister. Asta, according to Shaw, is the quiet, affectionate, enduring, reassuring, faithful, domestic temperament. Therefore Miss Robins relied on pathos, mute misery, and a certain delicate plaintive note in her voice which immediately gained the audience's sympathy. What Miss Robins obviously wanted to do was to present a complete contrast to the willful and passionate Rita.

Shaw concludes his review of *Little Eyolf* by putting himself into his old attitude as a music critic. He found the production as a whole to be unsatisfactory simply because all the performances were individual performances with no concern for the ensemble effect. What the production needed was a smoothly coordinated and carefully orchestrated performance. Miss Achurch, he felt, managed to play the second act as if she had been playing it every week for twenty years, but otherwise the play as a whole was unsatisfactory:

> If only the company could keep together for a while! But perhaps that is too much to hope for at present, though it is encouraging to see that the performances are to be continued next week, the five matinees—all crowded, by the way—having by no means exhausted the demand for places.[7]

The matinees were such a success that it had a boomerang effect on the fortunes of the Charringtons. A theatrical Syndicate, to Shaw, always the most evil of all capitalistic ventures, scented the possibilities of a fashionable success, and arranged a second production.

Mrs. Pat Campbell was elevated to the starring role of Rita Allmers, Miss Achurch was fired, and Elizabeth Robins retained in the role of Asta only because she owned the stage rights to the play. Shaw, in a bitter review of the second production hoped that the actresses involved made a lot of money out of their elevation to stardom—including Florence Farr who was engaged to replace Mrs. Campbell as the Ratwife, because otherwise the production was a complete disaster.

Mrs. Campbell entered thoroughly into the spirit of the fashionable alterations. She had seen how unlady-like, how disturbing, how full of horror the part of Rita Allmers was as acted by Miss Achurch. Now she succeeded in eliminating all the unpleasantness from the play. Her dresses were beyond reproach, her performance was infinitely reassuring and pretty. It was as if she had said:

> You silly people: what are you making all this fuss about? The secret of life is charm and self-possession, and not tantrums about drowned children. . . . And how nicely Mrs. Campbell took the drowning of the child! Just a pretty waving of the fingers, a moderate scream as if she had very nearly walked on a tin tack, and it was all over, without tears, without pain, without more fuss than if she had broken the glass of her watch.[8]

In his bitterness Shaw did not even find kind words for his old friend Florence Farr in the role of the Ratwife vacated by Mrs. Campbell. Once again, he felt she was inadequate and lacked the "sustained grip in the execution" of her role. She had several times as an occasional actress been rather successful and she might do this again if she could find time enough to spare from her other interests to take up acting seriously.

Nor did Miss Robins fare better from this angry critic. One of the difficulties of this cheap edition of the play was that Asta, instead of being the tranquilizing element became the center of the disturbance. The conduct of Allmers in turning from his pretty, coaxing, soothing wife to his agitated, high-strung sister was now nonsensical. In the first production Miss Robins had succeeded in making Asta a peacemaker since beside Miss Achurch she easily seemed gentle and understanding; beside Mrs. Campbell she seemed to be a volcano.

Shaw took some grim satisfaction in the fact that the new *Little Eyolf* was not a success, hampered as it was by the fact that it appeared before Mrs. Campbell even had time to learn her part. In the third act she had quite frankly stopped acting and brought the book on the stage to read from it. The failure of the production served those monsters of the professional theatre quite justly. They had turned a powerful domestic tragedy into a pleasant little domestic drama, "Ibsen without Tears," as Shaw entitled his review. They deserved to fail.

The Demise of the Independent Theatre:
The Birth of the Stage Society

It was quite understandable that Janet Achurch should feel betrayed by the lessees of the Avenue Theatre when they replaced her with Mrs. Pat Campbell. Mrs. Campbell had apparently offered to play Rita Allmers for a share in lieu of a salary. Janet's reaction was to retire to the Solferino Cafe near the Avenue Theatre between the last matinee and evening performances of *Little Eyolf.* Shaw suggested to his future wife, Charlotte Townsend, that she take Janet in hand. Miss Townsend, having been told by a colleague that the worst was happening, went to the Solferino Cafe, "yanked Janet (who was half dead) out of it, took her to Adelphi Terrace, put her to bed, and delivered her punctually in magnificent condition for the performance."[9] The Charringtons's mismanagement of the finances of the Independent Theatre, however, shortly afterward put that organization in further jeopardy.

Miss Achurch was engaged by Louis Calvert to play with him in *Antony and Cleopatra* in Manchester beginning March 20, 1897. Shaw dutifully went up to see it but did not report very favorably in the *Saturday Review.* As always, Shaw felt that the "music" was what was most important in any Shakespeare play, and here Janet had ideas of her own:

> The march of the verse and the strenuousness of the rhetoric stimulate her great artistic susceptibility powerfully: she is determined that Cleopatra shall have rings on her fingers and bells on her toes, and that she shall have music wherever she goes. Of the hardihood of ear with which she carries out her original and often audacious conceptions of Shakespearean music I am too utterly unnerved to give any adequate description. The lacerating discord of her wailings is in my tormented ears as I write, reconciling me to the grave.[10]

Mr. Calvert was decidedly overweight, which is perhaps why he decided to play Antony for comedy. This Shaw did not feel was a bad idea since his features were so pleasant, his manner so easy, his humor so genial and tolerant, and his portliness so frank and unashamed that no good-natured woman could resist him. No wonder that a few years later Shaw would want him for Tom Broadbent in the Court Theatre's *John Bull's Other Island*. But it did bring about a production in which Cleopatra was tragic in her comedy and Antony comedic in his tragedy.

This was all very well for Manchester but what was now unforgivable was that Janet wanted to appear as Cleopatra in London. Without consulting the stockholders of the Independent Theatre, the Charringtons produced *Antony and Cleopatra* at the Olympic on May 24, 1897. Shaw greeted this betrayal of the Independent Theatre's great tradition of producing plays which were impossible to do in the commercial theatres with a howl of anguish. Miss Achurch, however, wanted the London exposure in a Shakespearean role since all of her recent performances had been in modern plays. The exposure, according to Shaw had not added to her reputation. He, at least, had had an afternoon of anguish, spent partly in contemplating Miss Achurch's overpowering experiments in rhetoric, and partly in wishing he had never been born.

Shaw had spent many hours "schoolmastering Janet in the beautiful, quietly expressive, infinitely inflectionable normal voice" and she had been making progress. Now she had deliberately chosen a play which required another style of acting and one in which she was not well-trained. Miss Achurch some ten years before had played Shakespeare in the companies of both Frank Benson and Herbert Beerbohm Tree. But these popular actors had apparently not taught her the right way of delivering Shakespeare's speeches. At least it was not Shaw's way.

In this review of *Antony and Cleopatra* Shaw has a great deal to say about the art of rhetorical acting, of which Henry Irving was a master. He even gives a brief history of Irving's progress in the art, beginning with a performance of Richelieu at which Shaw says he suffered horribly, the audience suffered horribly and, although a humane man (considering his profession of drama critic), he hoped the actor suffered horribly:

> For I knew what rhetoric ought to be, having tasted it in literature, music, and painting; and as to the stage, I had seen great Italians do it in the days when Duse, like Ibsen, had not arrived. After a long period of convalescence, I ventured again to the Lyceum and saw Hamlet. There was a change, Richelieu had been incessantly excruciating: Hamlet had only moments of violent ineptitude separated by lengths of dulness [sic]; and though I yawned, I felt none the worse next morning.[11]

But when years later he went to the Lyceum to see *The Lady of Lyons*, Irving was now magnificent. Shaw saw that he had mastered the rhetorical style at last. Later performances became "a miracle of the most elaborate class of this sort of acting. It was a hard-earned and well-deserved triumph; and by it his destiny was accomplished; the anti-Irvingites were confuted. . . ."

Of course Janet could discipline herself to learn to perform Shakespeare effectively:

> Now what Sir Henry Irving has done, for good or evil, Miss Janet Achurch can do too. If she is tired of being "an Ibsenite actress": and wants to be a modern Ristori, it is clear that the public will submit to her apprenticeship as humbly as they submitted to Sir Henry Irving's.[12]

But just as Irving had, by learning the rhetorical style, turned his back on the modern drama, so would she.

In spite of this betrayal of the ideals of the Independent Theatre, Shaw was still loyal to the Charringtons. At the stockholders meeting, when the financial affairs of the Independent Theatre were revealed, he so manipulated the proceedings that Charles was retained as director. The moment of truth, however, was at hand. The Charringtons wanted at long last to bring *Candida* into London. They had given it a single public performance in Aberdeen on July 30, 1897, when they were also appearing in the inevitable *Doll's House*. The next year they included it in the

Independent Theatre's last Manchester season. On both occasions, Charles played Morell against Shaw's wishes. Shaw
had written him a long letter to the effect that Candida was
Janet's part, Morell was not his. He refused to let them
bring the play to London. This was the kiss of death for the
Independent Theatre. Another organization was shortly to
take its place in the London scene. This was the Stage
Society which was to function on slightly different lines
than the Independent Theatre. It was founded in 1899 by
Mr. Frederick Whelen. The Society's first performance,
given on November 22, 1899, was of Shaw's *You Never Can
Tell*.

The original purpose of the members of the Stage
Society was to form a club which would present plays nor-
mally forbidden production by the Lord Chamberlain's office. The plays were given on Sunday nights, thus enabling
actors who were professionally involved in commercial
productions to contribute their services. Attendance at the
plays was for members only and even the critics had to sub-
scribe for their seats. Although many of the plays given
were censored plays, it was not very long before the Stage
Society was producing for one or two performances several
of the Shaw plays which had not been given before save in
single performances for purposes of obtaining a copyright.

After *You Never Can Tell*, the Stage Society produced
Candida. Shaw was impressed by the sincerity, insight and
passion of a young actor, Granville Barker, who played
Marchbanks. But disappointment is too weak a word for
what he felt watching Janet Achurch play the part he had
written for her six years before. His only recorded comment
was that she didn't play the part; she "kicked it about the
stage."

Two years later Miss Achurch created the part of Lady
Cicely Waynflete in *Captain Brassbound's Conversion* for
the Stage Society. In trying to act high comedy Shaw felt
she was once again attempting an acting style which she
had not yet mastered and she was treated to one of the last
acting lessons by the Pygmalion who was about to despair
of ever making his Galatea the greatest actress on the London stage:

There is no doubt that you did, in a sort, begin to act high comedy for the first time in your life in the sense of carefully composing a picture instead of merely looking into a mirror in a volcanic manner, and saying: There! there's your Nora, Candida, etc. And you were so excited at finding the thing coming off, that each laugh produced the effect of a tablespoonful of brandy and soda; so that, if the graver touches had not brought you back to your seriousness, dignity, and power, you would finally have made Lady Cicely an exceptionally obstreperous maenad. . . . The fact is, you tumbled to the trick of comedy acting suddenly and luckily; . . . You can save the situation by falling back, in *my* plays, where the opportunities are mixed and the comedy tissue is shot with reality and tragedy, on the great Janet; but in a St. James's fashionable comedy you wouldn't get the chance. And that is why you would not suit the St. James's, because your comedy is not delicate enough, your parts not studied enough, and your heavy qualities not wanted.

Before you can play Lady Cicely perfectly, you will have to do what the author did, and do it much more minutely and personally than he: that is, make a careful study of the English lady. . . .[13]

Although she was cast as Vivie Warren in *Mrs. Warren's Profession* for the Stage Society, difficulties in procuring a theatre postponed the production, and the part was eventually played by Madge McIntosh. Shaw's friendship with the Charringtons continued until Janet's death in 1916 at the age of fifty-two, but they were never again associated professionally. The Charringtons played in the provinces from time to time but it was rumored that she was suffering from consumption, a rumor that was carefully encouraged by her friends. Shaw had at long last become convinced that she was not the right actress for his plays. The wonder is that he continued to believe for such a long time that she ever could play in them. She was apparently a great actress when she could appear in parts requiring volcanic energy and smouldering passion; there were few such parts in Shaw's plays.

Shaw would have been spared almost a decade of hard work with Janet Achurch if he had taken his mother's good advice in 1889. In his first letter to Janet on the occasion of the historic first night of *A Doll's House*, Shaw quotes to her Mrs. Shaw's remark to her son about Janet: "that one is a divil." "Divil" she was, and Shaw played John the Baptist to her Salome for all too many years. He kept his promise to Janet that *Candida* was her play up to and through the Stage Society's performance in 1900. If he had let Ellen Terry have it when she was asking him for a "mother play" in 1896 Shaw might have conquered West End audiences long before he did.

Shaw and Barker at the Court Theatre

The Stage Society had brought Shaw to the attention of its distinguished membership; but in 1904, the forty-eight-year-old playwright still had never had his plays produced for public evening performances in London save for Florence Farr's *Arms and the Man* production a decade before. The man who was finally to bring Shaw to the playhouses of London was Granville Barker. At the age of ninety, Shaw was to recall the Barker of 1900:

> In looking about for an actor suitable for the part of the poet in *Candida* at a Stage Society performance, I had found my man in a very remarkable person named Harley Granville-Barker. He was at that time 23 years of age, and had been on the stage since he was 14. He had a strong strain of Italian blood in him, and looked as if he had stepped out of a picture by Benozzo Gozzoli. He had a wide literary culture and a fastidiously delicate taste in every branch of art. He could write in a difficult and too precious but exquisitely fine style. He was self-willed, restlessly industrious, sober, and quite sane. He had Shakespeare and Dickens at his finger ends. Altogether the most distinguished and incomparably the most cultivated person whom circumstances had driven into the theatre at that time.[14]

Granville Barker at twenty-three had learned a great deal about the London theatre and had developed unbelievable ambitions. He had learned the new way of producing Shakespeare from William Poel and had developed tremendous admiration for this great innovator

who was to bring back the beauty of Shakespeare's
language to a theatre which had buried it for years under
massive sets. Thirty years later Barker was to pay tribute to
Poel as a director, but at the time he resented, as did other
actors, his tyranny. At one rehearsal of *Richard II*, according
to Poel's biographer Robert Speight, Poel locked the actors
in a room and threatened to keep them there until they had
learned his inflections. They were there most of the night.
Barker was to be almost as rigorous a taskmaster at the
Court Theatre. Shaw, who believed in three-hour rehearsals
from after breakfast to lunch, was to say that a Factory Act
for actors was needed at the Court Theatre, for Barker kept
them many times until they had missed their trains and
buses and he had tired himself beyond human powers of
maintaining the intense vigilance and freshness which first-
rate production demands.

Barker at one time had divided his life into ten years
for acting, ten years for producing, and ten years for
playwriting. Since he had begun as a child actor, his ten
years as an actor were up when he began acting Shaw. The
unbelievably useful and productive association with Shaw
at the Court Theatre allowed him to extend his time as an
actor and at the same time to begin his ten years as
producer and director. He even, at Shaw's insistence, was
shortly to begin his career as a playwright.

Before the Court Theatre opened its doors on April 26,
1904, Barker had approached William Archer with the idea
of a national repertory theatre. On April 21, 1903, he had
written a long letter to Archer setting out a proposal to take
the Court Theatre for six months or a year and run there a
stock season of the noncommercial drama. This would be
more or less continuing what the Stage Society had been
doing, but these productions would be extended to
weekday evenings as well as matinees. It was to be a subscription theatre, the highest prices charged being five or
six shillings; and there would be new productions every
fortnight.

Nothing came of this project for some little time, and
when it came into being it was in quite a different way.
J. H. Leigh, a businessman but also an enthusiastic actor

and Shakespeare buff, took a lease on the Court Theatre. He wanted to put on a series of Shakespeare productions, and these started on October 26, 1903, with *The Tempest*, in which Leigh played Caliban and his wife (and one-time ward) Thyrza Norman played Miranda. After a second Shakespeare presentation, Leigh was dissatisfied with what was being done and went with his wife to consult William Archer, who immediately told them to get Granville Barker to direct their next play. This they did, and Barker consented to do *Two Gentlemen of Verona*, providing he was permitted to put on matinees of Shaw's *Candida*. This concession was granted and *The Two Gentlemen of Verona* was a distinct success, with Barker playing Speed, Miss Norman playing Julia, and a young actor by the name of Lewis Casson playing Eglamour. This was to result in many years of friendship and professional association. It was the beginning of the nucleus of players who were to appear in thirty-two plays before Barker and Vedrenne left the Court Theatre for the Savoy on June 29, 1907.

Shortly after the production of *Two Gentlemen of Verona*, Leigh dropped out of the picture, but his business manager J. E. Vedrenne stayed on, and thus the Vedrenne-Barker Management was created. Shakespeare was now completely abandoned and his place as dramatist was now taken by Bernard Shaw. Barker had always wanted to repeat his role of Marchbanks in *Candida*, and now the production featured Kate Rorke as Candida and Norman McKinnel as Morell; the matinees started on April 26 while the *Two Gentlemen of Verona* was still running. In spite of Shaw's warning to Barker that the production would be a "hideous folly," it was instead a tremendous success and soon went into the evening bill.

Thus it was that twentiety-century English drama came into being in the small (it seated only 614) Court Theatre adjoining Sloane Square station on the Metropolitan District Railway. Although it was far from the West End hub of the professional theatre, the Court was ideal for the Vedrenne-Barker management since it was located between the districts of Chelsea and South Kensington where many Stage Society members lived.

Although it could never be said that they did not have their failures, the Court Theatre appealed to an audience that could forgive it failures in anticipation of future successes.

In the meantime a new personality entered the picture in the person of Gilbert Murray, the classical scholar and translator. Barker had produced his version of Euripides' *Hippolytus* for the New Century Theatre on May 26. It had been a great success, and several producers wished to take over the play. One of these was William Poel, and in sending on a letter from him to Murray, Barker enclosed the following advice:

> If I may advise, I wouldn't let him do it in London—for he may produce it in rather a cracked though clever way—not that what is so much a business reason as that there well may be a London revival in it as done just now. Also I'd be very sharp over your contract with him—for Poel is one of these limpid-eyed enthusiasts who sacrifices himself body, soul and pocket to his cause and is absolutely unscrupulous in making everyone else do the same thing.[15]

As a result of Barker's suggestions, the Vedrenne-Barker partnership was able to secure the *Hippolytus* for what was actually their first production on matinees beginning October 18, 1904. The partnership agreement, however, was not actually drawn up until the first regular evening performances of *John Bull's Other Island* on May 1 of the following year. The capital was to consist of "such sums of money as shall be required" for carrying on the business, and to be contributed by each partner in equal shares, but no sum was mentioned. The partners were to share equally in the profits or losses and were entitled to draw £20 a week each in anticipation of profits. Vedrenne was to be responsible for the business management and Barker for the artistic management. Shaw was not a partner, although it was obvious even then that his plays were to provide the greatest revenue at the box office and for this, as always, he was to be paid 10 percent of the gross in royalties.

John Eugene Vedrenne was at the time thirty-seven years of age and had been in theatrical management for some years. He had met Barker earlier when managing the

Comedy Theatre, and at that time had developed some interest in the so-called new drama. How much he knew about it has never been ascertained, but at least he was willing to take a chance on the hitherto unproduced Bernard Shaw as well as the Greek translations of Gilbert Murray. He was as unusual a businessman in the theatre as Barker was an actor; for in a partnership where there was so little capital, meticulous care had to be taken in budgeting the productions. Only £200 was allotted to each production and part of the Court Theatre's continued existence was due to the fact that he rigorously kept Barker within that budget.

A company of actors whose names included Lewis Casson, Norman Page, Edmund Gwenn, Trevor Lowe, Allan Wade, Dorothy Minto, and Mary Barton among others, could now be engaged. They were paid the ridiculously low salary of £3 a week, but it must be remembered that for part of the first year plays were produced only for three matinees a week. This meant the members of the company were free to accept evening employment in the West End. Similarly, some outstanding and relatively established actors could be brought in to fill out the casts. For instance, perhaps at Shaw's suggestion, Florence Farr played for two weeks in November, 1904, in Maeterlinck's *Aglavoine and Selysette* and was the chorus leader in Murray's translation of *The Trojan Women* in April of the next year.

The first production of *John Bull's Other Island*, Shaw's first new play for the Court, was for matinees beginning November 1, 1904, and it became an immediate success; even Beatrice Webb liked it, and with the new political influence which the Fabian Society was able to wield, Prime Minister A. J. Balfour, as well as the Leader of the Opposition Sir Henry Campbell-Bannerman, made his appearance at the Court Theatre. It was revived beginning February 7, 1905, and a special performance was given on the evening of March 29 for His Majesty Edward VII. One of the legends of the Court is that he laughed so hard that he fell off the chair which the management had borrowed, and broke it. Shaw thought he ought to be charged for the

damage, but, indeed, the Court Theatre had now become
the Royal Court.

The production of *John Bull's Other Island* was not as
easy as its immediate success would lead one to believe.
The play is primarily a contrast of two opposing male leads,
Tom Broadbent, the Englishman, and Larry Doyle, the
Irishman. At Shaw's insistence, Louis Calvert, whom Shaw
remembered as a chubby Antony opposite Janet Achurch's
Cleopatra, was cast as Broadbent since he was a fine come-
dian and could make the romantic but practical
Englishman believable. W. L. Shine won the part of Larry
Doyle, the disillusioned Irishman. Ellen O'Malley, who was
to become one of Shaw's favorite actresses at the Court,
played Nora. Granville Barker persuaded Shaw to let him
play Father Keegan, the unfrocked priest. This cameo role,
so important to the play, was small enough to allow him to
help Shaw with the direction and do what he could do so
well: pull the entire cast along with him when the other
performances seemed to be going to pieces.

John Bull's Other Island was also the first play to be
put on in the evenings for a three weeks' engagement,
beginning May 1, 1905. It had become such a success that
by the fall it was given for an unprecedented six weeks. At
this time Louis Calvert was still playing his original role of
Tom Broadbent, but Ben Webster (once of the Lyceum
Company) had replaced W. L. Shine as Larry Doyle, and
William Poel, Barker's one-time mentor, now replaced him
as Father Keegan.

Thus with the success of the matinees of *Candida* in
the spring, what could be called the Shaw-Barker
partnership was really launched at the Court. Shaw always
produced his own plays with Barker's help in the capacity of
what now might be called stage manager. Barker produced
all the plays by other authors with much counsel and comment from Shaw on their choice, their casting, and their
style.

The fame of this Shaw-Barker partnership was such
that a legend grew up that Granville Barker was Shaw's son,
although no mother was ever mentioned. One biographer
attributes it to a remark made by Barker to Shaw during a

rehearsal that Shaw was old enough to be his father. When St. John Ervine first heard of it he suggested to his informant that "the strongest refutal of it was G.B.S.'s failure to boast about it, as he certainly would have done had it been true."[16]

Shaw and Barker on Stage

The partnership that evolved between Shaw and Barker for the production of plays at the Court Theatre was a unique combination of backgrounds and abilities. Shaw had spent thousands of hours in the auditoriums of theatres; Barker had spent thousands of hours on stage in rehearsal and in performance. Each learned a great deal from the other.

Quite probably Barker learned from Shaw the importance of treating a play as if it were a symphony and the actors as if they were the instruments in an orchestra. Shaw, who had almost no experience as an actor, probably learned from Barker ways of communicating with actors and helping them to understand the subtleties of interpretation.

Proof of the extent of Shaw's indebtedness to his younger colleague was found by Bernard Dukore for his book *Bernard Shaw Director*. It is contained in a letter from the Hanley Collection to W. L. Shine, when *John Bull's Other Island* was being produced for the first time at the Court. Shine was having trouble with his big speech in the first act of the play in which as Larry Doyle the Irishman he is telling Tom Broadbent the Englishman of the Irishman's fatal penchant for dreaming and not doing.

Professor Dukore, himself a one-time director as well as a distinguished Shaw scholar, points out that Shaw told Shine how to break up a long and difficult speech in several ways. He gave the actor an explanatory paraphrase, physical business (a shiver of disgust and a nervous fidget), subtext ('a sort of half tender reproach'), literary analysis (poetry, prose, and description), and inner feeling (shame when he remembers what he himself did). Shaw thus separated the speech into distinct units, not just in motivational terms but in such a way that it was given variety and the actor was assisted in giving the illusion that he was formulating his thoughts step by step to another living character instead of repeating mechanically a set speech.

As time went on Barker and Shaw's partnership (for such it really was) became such that there was an instinctive agreement on many things. When it came to acting styles, however, there was one important difference of opinion. Barker, although a Shakespearean actor and director, when acting in modern plays many times used the low-key approach of the Tom Robertson "cup and saucer" school of playwrighting and acting. Shaw heartily disliked this approach. Its realism, freely daubed with Victorian sentiment, was certainly pallid compared to Ibsen's realism. In reading Robertson's plays today one is impressed by the fact that there are more stage directions than dialogue. In fact, it has been said that Robertson's plays could be comprehended if the actors said nothing. To Shaw, this was a horror. Opera, yes; ballet and pantomime, no! Shaw was to say over and over again that actors could play on the line, over the line, and under the line, but never, never, *between* the lines. Barker, accustomed to the subtleties of the new realism, still felt that sometimes this was necessary.

This is the reason for Shaw's criticism of Barker for hiring actors who were not "stagey" enough: "Keep your worms for your own plays and leave me the drunken, stagey, brass boweled barnstormers my plays are written for."[17] The "worms" were all very well also for the continental plays which Barker was directing for the Court, but Shaw's plays, he tells him, are really variety entertainment, "a series of turns." On the other hand if he would only get his cast right, stage management would take care of itself.

When it came to casting, Barker usually deferred to Shaw's judgment, since he realized that not only did the solvency of the Court require Shaw's plays, but that during his years as a critic, Shaw had seen most of the important actors at work. He had kept a filing system of these actors, and there were elaborate notes on not only important actors but also any others with whom he was impressed. At one point Shaw, when they were casting *Hedda Gabbler*, gave Barker the names of the actors he thought could play the male roles, listing sixteen names for Tesman, twenty-two for Judge Brack, and eight for Lovborg—but with five understudies. It is small wonder Barker was bewildered!

It is a commonplace of theatre criticism that the nineteenth century was the century of the great actor; that it was followed by fifty years when the great playwrights were in their ascendancy; and that our theatre of today is a director's theatre. It was Shaw and Barker who actually did nore than anyone in their time in England to elevate the director to a position of importance. Shaw made several important statements and summaries of his method of directing a play. One of the earliest of these was a letter written in 1922 to his old friend of Dublin days, Matthew McNulty, in response to a request for advice and information. It was later reprinted under several titles, although the one used most frequently is "The Art of Rehearsal."

Almost a quarter of a century later, in 1949, Shaw was to write another summary of his method of staging a play called "Rules for Directors." A great part of this article repeats the same steps as those outlined in "The Art of Rehearsal." Here, however, Shaw really is describing his own activities as author-director. At the age of ninety he seems to be remembering with nostalgia those exciting, creative hours in the dusty, dingy, drafty, uncomfortable Court Theatre.

Shaw summarizes his method in a few well worked-out steps requiring four weeks of rehearsal. On the first day there would be a careful reading of the play to the entire cast by the director. Next there would be a week devoted to blocking with the actors on stage with the director, reading their parts but not attempting to act. At this point it is very important, Shaw says, to have all actors exactly placed for their important speeches and also to have them near their exits as well as near hats and canes and anything else they must take with them. This procedure is repeated for about a week until the actors know all their exits, entrances, and places on the stage. They are then sent home to learn their parts and at the beginning of the second week there is what Shaw calls a "perfect rehearsal"—meaning a run-through without scripts. He warns that at this time there will be

innumerable mistakes, only the grossest of which should be
corrected.

After this there are two weeks of rehearsal when there
is no one on the stage but the actors, since the director sits
at the back of the house with a flashlight taking copious
notes. These are privately given to the performers, for no
corrections are made before the other members of the cast.
Shaw estimates that he had 600 notes for the members of
the cast of *Arms and The Man*. Later his notes would run
into the thousands for a play which he was directing from
beginning to end. So far the time elapsed has been about
four weeks and the company is now ready for a week of
dress rehearsal. By this time the actors should know more
about their parts in the play than even the director-
playwright. Still Shaw expected many flaws to remain; he
even liked a final dress rehearsal to go badly; it put the actors on their mettle for the opening.

Although he had far more respect for human
limitations than did Barker, who drove himself and his casts
to the point of exhaustion, Shaw also made extraordinary
demands. Having decided to cast Louis Calvert as Andrew
Undershaft for the world première of *Major Barbara*, Shaw
immediately sent him a directive telling him to procure a
trombone and learn to play it on his vacation. He tells him
that learning to play a wind instrument will be beneficial to
his health since he would have to give up the dreadful
cigars which were ruining his voice and his memory. He is
warned that the part is a tremendous one with speeches
requiring infinite nuances of execution:

> Undershaft is diabolically subtle, gentle, selfpossessed,
> powerful, stupendous, as well as amusing and interesting.
> There are the makings of ten Hamlets and six Othellos in his
> mere leavings. Learning it will half kill you; but you can
> retire the next day as pre-eminent and unapproachable.[18]

But Shaw tempts Calvert to accept the role with the kind
of flattery usually reserved for actresses; Irving and Beerbohm, he predicts, will fade from the memory of playgoers
when Calvert takes the stage as Sir Andrew Undershaft.

Calvert accepted the part, but found it to be even more

difficult than had been anticipated. Shaw wrote to him after the rehearsal of November 17, 1905:

> I hope I did not worry you too much today at rehearsal. The fact is you are ruining the end of the second act by your enormous, desolating, oblivious-to-everybody absent-mindedness. The reason I put on an understudy for Barbara was that you had driven Miss Russell almost out of her senses by letting the scene drop when she was doing her hardest to get hold of it. She did not complain; but I saw what was happening and acted on my own initiative. You see, it is all very well for you; you know that you can wake up at the last moment and do the trick; but that will not help out the unhappy victims who have to rehearse with you. And you forget your own weight. The moment you let the play go, it drops.[19]

There was only one more week of rehearsals, and Shaw was afraid that Calvert, on whom the entire second act depended, would let the whole play down. The whole movement of the act was charged by what Shaw calls "his colossal indifference." The other actors were affected by this indifference and Miss Russell as Major Barbara had almost given up in despair. Shaw ends this note with an admission that the part is a heroic one and that there was a tremendous lot for Calvert to learn, but that words were not strong enough to describe what he was doing to the second act:

> . . . you will scream through endless centuries in hell for it, and implore me in vain to send you ices from heaven to cool your burning tongue. We have only one week more; and I have set my heart on your making a big success in the part. And you are taking it as easy as if Undershaft were an old uncle in a farce. Spend tomorrow in prayer. My wife was horrified at my blanched hair and lined face when I returned from rehearsal today. And I have a blinding headache and can [say] no more.[20]

When the play opened, Shaw was incensed by the fact that Calvert had gotten excellent notices for his performance, but that *Major Barbara* had been called an undramatic play. He wrote to him that he still felt *Major Bar-*

bara was a masterpiece but that Calvert was at fault for the shortcomings of the performance. He tells him that any man who could let the famous "Seven Deadly Sins Speech" in the last act go for nothing could sit on a hat without making an audience laugh. He then gives him a warning that he has taken a box for Friday and had a hundred weight of cabbages, dead cats, eggs, and ginger beer bottles stacked under it:

> . . . Every word you fluff, every speech you unact, I will shy something at you. Before you go on the stage I will insult you until your temper gets the better of your liver. You are an imposter, a sluggard, a blockhead, a shirk, a malingerer, and the worst actor that ever lived or that ever will live. I will apologize to the public for engaging you. I will tell your mother of you. Barbara placed you off the stage; Cremlin dwarfed you; Bill annihilated you; Clare Greet took all eyes from you. If you are too lazy to study the lines I'll coach you in them. That last act MUST be saved or I'll withdraw the play and cut you off without a shilling.[21]

In "Rules for Directors" Shaw elaborates on how the notes for the actors actually are the test of a director's competence. If, for example, the notes read "Show influence of Kierkegaard on Ibsen in this scene," or "The Oedipus complex must be very apparent here, discuss with the Queen," the sooner he is packed out the theatre and replaced the better. If they run "Ears too red," "Further up to make room for X," "Pleecemin," "Reel and Ideel," "Mariar Ann," "He, no Ee," "Change speed: Andante," "Shoe sole arches not blacked," "Unladylike: keep knees together," and the like, the director knows his job and place.[22] In other words, the director who wants an actor to portray the "influence of Kierkegaard on Ibsen" is utterly impractical. The director who is giving his cast useful directives on makeup, diction, and posture will achieve tangible results.

Another of Shaw's practical methods of illustrating how a scene should be played was his habit of taking the actor aside and performing the scene with great exaggeration of both speech and action. This was deliberately done so that the actor would not imitate him but would only grasp the idea of the effect that was wanted. The actor should use

his own creativity to produce that effect. This is why Dame
Edith Evans later described Shaw as "an awful ham."[23] He
was, deliberately so, when he was illustrating what was
wanted in his plays.

Barker never left as definite and succinct a record as
did Shaw, but Sir Lewis Casson, who was directed by
Barker in many Court productions and who acted with him
in several Shaw plays, describes in the Foreword to the Purdom biography of Barker how nearly parallel their directorial methods were. Sir Lewis says that with Barker, too,
the first step was a reading of the entire play to the cast,
"more for its sense than for character or drama." There was
no "directorial jargon" or pretentious analysis. The second
step, which probably corresponds to Shaw's week on the
stage with the actors carrying their books but not attempting to memorize their parts, was what Barker calls
"molding the play."

Perhaps the most impressive thing about Barker's work
as a director was the attention he paid to the ensemble work
on the stage and the care given to small parts. The most important thing in the production was to evolve a unity of setting, voices, and movement to express the author's intent.
What Barker and Shaw both insisted upon was the rhythm
in a production, the repetition of the rise and fall of the action, the little variations which could produce a symphonic
effect. When working on a play, Barker would spend hours
at the pianola which the Shaws had given him for a wed-
ding present; from this he felt he could derive the rhythms
he wanted for a play.

At rehearsal he was wholly concentrated; he never
shouted or lost his temper. In the last stages of rehearsal he
would never go on-stage until the end of the play when he
would sometimes move the actors into more favorable
positions. Like Shaw, if he had detailed instructions for any
one actor, they would be given privately. He was never one
to praise performances; they simply had to be right, and to
be right they must be effortless. What Shaw and Barker
brought to the London theatre of their day was, above all,
an insistence on the importance of the play and the music in
it. Neither of them had any use for theatrical effects and

neither allowed anything to be done on the stage that was
simply "effective" unless whatever it was—intonation,
movement, gesture, look, timing, pause, or use of properties—belonged to the play or was necessary for its interpretation. Nothing in their plays was ever left to chance.

Lillah McCarthy Claims Her Kingdom

With casting and rehearsal techniques worked out, and
with *Candida* and *John Bull's Other Island* proving
successful in evening performances, Shaw now wanted to
see the play produced on which he had lavished more time
than any other up to this point. This was *Man and Superman* which had now been published, and Shaw was certain
that Barker could play Jack Tanner, its protagonist. There
was, however, no one in the company who could approach
the very difficult role of Ann Whitefield, who pursues this
modern Don Juan. In Shaw's version of the Don Juan
legend, he is an artist philosopher desperately trying to
avoid any romantic entanglement which will blunt the will
of the Life Force which is using him as its instrument to
create a superman with a philosopher's brain. Ann
Whitefield is relentless and unscrupulous, quite willing to
lie and cheat to gain her end—the husband whom the Life
Force tells her will be the best father for the child she wants
to bear. Such a young woman, unless she is vibrant with life
and irresistible in her beauty, could be distinctly unpleasant, and it required a very special young woman to play
her. One afternoon she appeared at Shaw's flat at Adelphi
Terrace in the person of Lillah McCarthy. Shaw greeted her
by saying, "Why here's Ann Whitefield."

Lillah McCarthy had played Lady Macbeth at the age
of fifteen and Shaw had written a favorable review telling
her to spend ten years learning her business as an actress.
Now, at twenty-five, she turned up in a "green dress and
outrageous picture hat" to tell Shaw that she had finished
her apprenticeship. He was so impressed by this young
woman, who had "the gait of a Diana and the voice of
Sarah Siddons," that he gave her the keys of her
kingdom—a copy of *Man and Superman*. She was told to go
home and study the part of Ann Whitefield.

Lillah McCarthy had spent the intervening ten years learning her craft. She had learned the new way of acting Shakespeare with William Poel; she had learned the old way on tour with the Ben Greet Company. She had toured the dominions with the actor-manager Wilson Barrett, playing Lady Mercia in *The Sign of the Cross.* Beginning as an understudy for the role, she had learned her lessons so well that on their return to England, Barrett wanted to send her out with a company of her own, playing Lady MacBeth, Phaedra, and Sudermann's Magda. Unfortunately, Wilson Barrett died shortly after this. Miss McCarthy took stock of her situation and realized that the romantic dramas of the Wilson Barrett school were passing out of fashion. The new realism indicated the temper of the times, and she realized that she must make a fresh start. She therefore presented herself to Shaw.

Lillah McCarthy's work at the Court Theatre did not actually begin with her creation of Ann Whitefield, but rather with acting Nora in a revival of *John Bull's Other Island.* Also, during an interlude before the production of *Man and Superman,* she went for part of the season to act with Beerbohm Tree at His Majesty's Theatre. It was, she says, like going away into another country; the atmosphere of the two theatres and the methods of the two producers were completely different: Shaw was serious, painstaking, concentrated, relentless in the pursuit of perfection. Tree used the "broader brush of the impressionists; casual, but full of inventiveness. . . . So once again I see-sawed between realism and romanticism. . . ."[24] Finally the anti-romantic *Man and Superman* without the dream scene began two weeks of matinees at the Court beginning May 23, and by the fall of 1905 it was produced evenings for three weeks.

It might have been some strange manifestation of the evolutionary appetite that brought Lillah McCarthy and Granville Barker together in *Man and Superman.* Acting Ann Whitefield and Jack Tanner in the throws of the Life Force on stage brought about a similar reaction to these young people off-stage. On April 24, 1906, they were married at the West Strand Registry Office (where the Shaws had been married in 1898). Shaw immediately

wrote to Vedrenne of his partner's marriage and frightened
him by intimating that now Lillah would have all the good
parts. It was greatly to Vedrenne's credit that he realized
the danger of such a situation. It is disastrous for the players
in a repertory company to feel that there is not going to be
open casting, and it would be difficult to keep actresses on
the payroll at three pounds a week if the best they could
hope for was second leads and a chance to understudy.
Lillah did indeed get to play many of the leads in the new
Shaw plays as well as the revivals which were continually
taking place. This, however, was more at Shaw's insistence
than her husband's. As will be seen, Shaw always wanted
both of the Barkers for his plays if they were available, and
Lillah was usually loyal to the Master-builder who had
presented her not only with a kingdom but with the crown
prince to boot.

Lillah McCarthy proved herself to be one of the most
satisfactory actresses ever to appear in Shaw's plays. As a little girl her father had sent her up into the hills of her native
Cheltenham to declaim Book II of *Paradise Lost*. This and
the subsequent years in the professional theatre had given
her a voice which could hold its own against "the stagey,
brass-boweled actors" Shaw wanted for his plays. His ap-
preciation of her talent was such that, although she was the
recipient of many corrective notes from him, they were
never quite the fulminations which Shaw directed at other
actors, including her husband.

Very shortly after their marriage Shaw finished the
third of the new plays for the Court Theatre, *The Doctor's
Dilemma*. It could almost be said that this play of a devoted
wife's effort to save her husband's life was written not only
for, but to some slight degree about, the Barkers. It was
produced on November 20, 1906, for eight matinees and
later entered the evening bill on December 31, 1906, for six
weeks. Purdom says that Shaw had Barker so definitely in
mind for the role of Louis Dubedat, the artist-philosopher,
that he even described Barker in his stage direction:
". . . although he is all nerves, and very observant and
quick of apprehension, he is not in the least shy . . . he
moves among men as most men move among things,

though he is intentionally making himself agreeable to them.''[25] Barker's performance was much criticized, although Desmond McCarthy, in writing the history of the Court Theatre, praised him for acting his death scene in the fourth act naturally and realistically, and defended him against the charge that he made the artist die "in a pose." After all, this was what Shaw intended.

The fifth act of this play, after the death of the artist, was Miss McCarthy's own. At an exhibition of the late artist's work his wife is autographing copies of the book she has written about him *The Artist as King*. Sir Colenso Ridgeon, the physician, who is responsible for his death because he denied him the serum that might have saved his life, is confronted by the widow. Shaw wrote to Lillah concerning the way she played it:

> . . . you have softened it out of existence. What I call the climax is Jennifer's discovery that Ridgeon deliberately murdered Dubedat. The dramatic effect is built up rather deliberately, because there is first a misunderstanding, and then a discovery. When Ridgeon first says "I killed him," the audience knows that he means "I murdered him"; but Jennifer thinks that her own frankness and sincerity have at last conquered his vanity, and that what he means is "Yes, yes, I own up. I confess I was a duffer and made a mess of the case." And on this she is delighted and forgives him.
>
> So far you seem to understand the scene clearly. What I think you miss is the force of the revulsion of feeling when she makes the appalling discovery that Louis was actually deliberately murdered. The point may be a little difficult because I have not done it in my usual way with a single stroke. She has to arrive at the truth by arguing about the medicines, being a little stupid and off the track at first, because the truth is so inconceivable and so wildly remote from her first misunderstanding. But when the revelation does come it really ought to be a blinding one. It has to be done on the line "It is only dawning on me, oh! oh! you MURDERED him." I think you try to get this effect on the soft tack instead of on the explosive one. That, of course, is often a very good way of pulling off a big effect; but in this case it misses fire. Also, the line goes wrong. The repeated exclamation which is put there to enable you to build up the

final thunder-clap becomes quite senseless. It does not belong to the soft way of doing it.

Next time just try the effect of letting yourself go on it for all you are worth, and keep up the transport of horror and incredulous amazement until you get his reply to your threat to kill him, which will let you down easily.[26]

From the time Lillah made her first appearance on the stage of the Court Theatre in *John Bull's Other Island*, she played most of Shaw's heroines for over a decade, and nearly always to his satisfaction. A last example of his confidence in her is a note written to her when Shaw had been told that she was to play the Strange Lady in *The Man of Destiny* in a private performance for King George at Number Ten Downing Street. Actually the third act of *John Bull's Other Island*, which had so amused King George's brother, was substituted but Shaw's advice to Lillah is revealing:

How are you getting on with the Strange Lady? Don't bother finessing about her: you won't get it that way. Play the downright aristocrat when the lady is not deliberately acting: go in for strength and beauty rather than for Lamballesque elegance. You haven't time to study a period: at such short notice all you can do is to fling on the stage a straight playing of the part in your own manner.[27]

Ellen Terry and Captain Brassbound

Shortly after the Barkers' marriage, the Royal Court Theatre was in financial straits. Several of the experimental matinees were failures and could not be continued in the evening bills. Shaw appeared on the scene to threaten bankruptcy again in a perhaps carefully calculated rage, and to make a suggestion. Ellen Terry, England's most beloved actress, was about to celebrate her jubilee of fifty years on the stage. Why should she not be invited to appear in *Captain Brassbound's Conversion*, the play Shaw had written for her almost a decade before?

Miss Terry had reversed an initial opinion that the play would not do for her, after hearing her touring company's copyright performance of it in Liverpool in 1898. But in

1902 the always loyal Ellen felt she should be available for Sir Henry Irving as the storm clouds gathered over the Lyceum, which was shortly to fall into the hands of those arch-villains, the members of the syndicate. For this reason she did not do the Stage Society's production at that time. Now, in 1906, she was, except for the Jubilee, without plans for the spring season and she accepted. Since it was her jubilee year and there was much attendant publicity, it was decided after the first matinee performance to put it on for an unprecedented twelve-week run throughout the rest of the spring. Although all this was in direct contradiction of the original Court policy of no West End stars and no long runs, there was a good reason to make an exception in the case of Ellen Terry.

Ellen Terry was not only a great actress, but she was also one of the most distinguished women of her day. Brooks Atkinson, in a review of her most recent biography by Roger Manville, entitles his review "Everybody Was In Love With Ellen," and he concludes his review by saying, "Since she was also beautiful, animated, modest, intelligent and gregarious it is no wonder everyone was in love with her—including her present biographer. The present reviewer, too."[28]

Her unassailable position in the English Theatre is all the more remarkable because of the irregularity of her early life. Her father and mother were well known in the acting profession. At the age of sixteen, Ellen had been married to the painter George Watts. The marriage was never consummated, and shortly afterward she began her acting career with considerable success. Estranged from her parents, she went to live with the architect Edward Godwin, who became the father of her two illegitimate children, Gordon and Edith, who later took the name of Craig. Godwin was unable to support her, and in 1874 she returned to the theatre in several plays by her old friend Charles Reade and eventually became leading lady to Henry Irving. During the years at the Lyceum, although never married to Irving, she was always his official hostess, frequent companion, and leading lady. (Irving was at this time estranged but not divorced from his wife.) Somehow, however, none of this irregular life style seemed to dim her popularity with Victorian audiences, and for thirty years she was the most popular actress of her day.

Captain Brassbound's Conversion was really not the first play Shaw had written about her. There is a great deal of Ellen Terry in the part of Candida. Although he was later to deny that the part was based on her personality, it called for the very quality which Shaw had seen in Ellen Terry's work on the stage. She created a personality which transcended all the roles which she played. In the portraits and photographs in the biographies of her, she seems always the same person, only the costume changes— whether Portia, Lady MacBeth, or Olivia in *The Vicar of Wakefield*.

Shaw was very pleased with *Candida* and believed that he had at last written a play worthy of her genius. Ellen Terry early expressed an interest in it and wanted to read it. Shaw refused at first saying "I never let people read that: I always read it to them. They can be heard sobbing three streets off." Finally he was prevailed upon to send her a script and she immediately wrote to him saying she had cried her eyes out over his *heavenly* play.

The Shaw-Terry story had begun before the composition of *Candida* when GBS was music critic for *The Star*. Ellen Terry, always trying to help young artists, had written the editor asking for some publicity for a young singer at whose concert she was to recite. Shaw, as music critic, not only reviewed the concert, but also took it upon himself to write Ellen the first of many letters. It is typical that in the letter he told her that he did not feel that her protégée had much talent, but that Ellen's recitation of a very trivial poem proved that she was a great artist.

Not too long afterward Shaw became the drama critic of the *Saturday Review*, and the letters became more and more frequent. At no time was there any suggestion on the part of either of them that they should meet in person. As a veteran of many a dressing-room interview, Shaw perhaps realized the danger of meeting in person an actress who was nine years older than he, since such a meeting might be disastrous for the romantic attachment which he had by now developed for her; but by 1897 Miss Terry's letters were eagerly awaited. Ellen, too, expressed much interest in him and even by this time was suggesting somewhat indirectly that they meet. She had become very curious about the life of London's most eligible bachelor critic. In typical Shaw fashion he warns her that he is never serious in his flirtations and that "his pockets are always filled with the small change of love." Ellen learned about his complicated relationship with Janet Achurch and the friendship that was developing with his fellow Fabian, Miss Charlotte Payne-Townshend, who was by now doing much of his typing. On June 1, 1898, he married Miss Payne-Townshend and resigned his position on the *Saturday Review* because of a serious illness. Miss Terry immediately sent her congratulations to them both and after Shaw's recovery the correspondence continued for many years.

The play *Captain Brassbound's Conversion* was based on a novel published in 1883 by George Rowe and Augustus Harris called *Captain Brassbound's Freedom*. There were many examples in the Victorian theatre of what was then called the adventure melodrama. North Africa was a favorite setting for this kind of play, probably because of the popularity of Ouida's romance *Under Two Flags* (1867). There were at least half a dozen such plays, all with the same ingredients. A beautiful European woman is introduced into a savage and barbaric background of villainous Arabs. The beleaguered English or French garrison is threatened and captured. The woman is coveted by the Arab leader for his harem, but is eventually rescued by a heroic representative of that "thin red line of heroes" who defend the empire.

Obviously a Fabian socialist deeply opposed to Imperialism had to turn this inside out, although Shaw uses all the basic ingredients of capture and rescue. His Captain Brassbound presents himself and his followers as an escort to Sir Howard Hallam and his sister-in-law Lady Cicely Wayneflete who wish to venture into the untamed vastness of the Moroccan mountains. Brassbound's motive, however, is actually to revenge himself on Sir Howard who is really his uncle and who, Brassbound believes, has years before

wronged his mother and deprived him of his rightful in-
heritance. Captain Brassbound's plan works perfectly and
they are at his mercy.

Now, of course, Shaw's Lady Cicely, with charm, tact,
and kindness, persuades Captain Brassbound to forego his
revenge. Shaw establishes a nice balance between the law
of England and the law of the Atlas Mountains, between
the justice of Brassbound and the justice of Sir Howard.
The party is rescued at the end of the second act and the
question now arises: Will Captain Brassbound be spared in
the court-martial which will take place after their return to
civilization? Shaw, who had greatly admired Ellen in the
trial scene of *The Merchant of Venice*, now created,
therefore, two trial scenes for Lady Cicely, whose character,
one critic thinks, was based on Shelly's Witch of Atlas. (This
was, indeed, the original title of the play.) Lady Cicely in-
duces a new spirit of compassion in Captain Brassbound,
and in the last act is able again through her ingenuous tact
and charm to produce the same effect on Sir Howard and so
rescue Captain Brassbound. She also has inspired in him a
new self-confidence to replace the old code of fear, aggres-
sion, and revenge. At the end of the play Captain
Brassbound begs her to depart with him as his
"commander-in-chief." Lady Cicely, however, although
somewhat tempted, persuades him that he must accomplish
and implement his new purpose in the world without her.

Unfortunately, on first reading Ellen Terry didn't like
the play at all and didn't fancy herself in the part of Lady
Cicely. "I don't think this play of yours will do for me at
all," she writes in one letter and continues in her next, "I
don't like the play one bit. Only *one* woman in it. How *ugly*
it will look, and there will not be a penny in it."[29] This was a
great blow to Shaw, who was gentleman enough not to tell
her that the reason there was only one woman in the play
was that he did not feel Miss Terry, at the age of fifty, could
compete with a stage full of younger actresses. Shaw's
answer to all of her objections is a rather moving one. He
writes to her on August 4, 1899:

> Alas, dear Ellen, is it really so? Then I can do nothing for
> you. I honestly thought that Lady Cicely would fit you like a

glove, that I had sacrificed everything to make the play go effectively from second to second, even that Drinkwater was a tragi-comic figure worthy of Robson. And now you tell me it is a play for the closet, and that Lady Cicely would suit Mrs. P. C.—all of which proves that either I am mad, or you are mad, or else there is an impassable gulf between my drama and your drama. I won't suggest it to Mrs. Pat because I am now quite convinced that she would consider herself born to play it, just as you want to play Cleopatra. No: it is clear that I have nothing to do with the theatre of to-day: I must educate a new generation with my pen from childhood up—audience, actors and all, and leave them my plays to be murdered after I am cremated. Captain B. shall not be profaned by the stage: I will publish it presently. . . .[30]

Now, seven years later, Ellen consented to create Lady Cicely Wayneflete, and Shaw wrote to her triumphantly:

I am looking forward with malicious glee to the rehearsals. I shall have my revenge then. I will not leave a rag, not a wink, not a flipperty top of that tiresome Ellen Terry who would not do my play.[31]

When it actually came to rehearsals Shaw disregarded his usual policy of keeping a firm hold. Face to face with Ellen he became strangely diffident and turned most of the direction over to Barker. Instead of the usual notes to the actors, he wrote to Barker when it became obvious the production was in trouble. Ellen was having difficulty remembering her lines:

Do not let Ellen repeat any scene. When she gets through she always wants to do it over and over again until it is right. There are two fatal objections. 1. She always goes to pieces the second time and discourages and demoralizes herself more and more every time. 2. She has just strength to get through the play once without tiring herself before lunch; and the repetition of a scene means a corresponding omission at the end. Go straight through and don't let them stop for anything. In any case the policy of sticking at it until we get it is a vulgar folly. Let them take their failure and the shame of it home and they will think about it and pull it off next time.[32]

At another rehearsal, Theodore Stier, the musical director, overheard Vedrenne incredulously asking Shaw if Miss Terry was actually speaking his lines on the stage. "No," said Shaw chivalrously, "she is speaking the lines I should have written."[33] The result was that on the opening night the play lacked Shaw's sureness of touch and Desmond McCarthy in his review actually preferred the 1902 Stage Society's production with Janet Achurch.

Ellen's jubilee, which took place on April 28, 1906, on the stage of the Drury Lane Theatre, was a great success. Twenty-four members of the Terry family appeared with her and the subscription audience contributed between 5,000 and 6,000 pounds. Unfortunately *Captain Brassbound* at the Royal Court did not begin to live up to the fond hopes of the author as a means of sustaining the failing fortunes of the theatre. Shaw gallantly blamed the play, rather than Miss Terry.

Shaw had captured the personality of Ellen Terry so well in the role that she was to complain to him later that she wished some playwright would write a part for her to act. "In this play of yours I have nothing to do but go on stage and be myself, and the thing is done." It was as far as her part was concerned, but the play itself is one of the few Shaw plays that is primarily a one-character play. As such, Lady Cicely is one of Shaw's great creations because of the woman who was her prototype:

> She is the spirit of woman as it is found, mischieviously or benignly, through all Shaw's *oeuvre*. She is also Shaw's idea of an actress—though this expression is too abstract to suggest the kind of inspiration which a creator of great roles for women can draw from a woman playing great roles.[34]

The financial failure of *Captain Brassbound* was not Ellen's fault. She long ago had said that her public was not ready for the play. They were loyal to her as long as they could go to see her in the West End in proximity to the luxury restaurants for their after-theatre suppers. They would not take the trouble to go to Sloan Square and the shabby little Queen's Restaurant.

Shaw permitted Ellen to take *Captain Brassbound* on

tour to the United States where it opened at the Empire Theatre in New York on January 28, 1907. Although it did not play at a financial loss, the New York critics did not give Miss Terry the enthusiastic reviews she had always had when she played in Shakespeare. On her return to England she continued to tour with it in the suburbs; and Shaw went to see her for one last time when she was playing in Fulham. His only comment was that Ellen Terry had at last succeeded in becoming Lady Cicely. It was, perhaps, the best instance of an actress achieving Shaw's desired "metaphysical self-realization."

From the Court to the Savoy

Early in 1907 Barker had once again produced several experimental plays at matinees, none of which proved to be successful. One of these was John Masefield's play, *The Campden Wonder*, and although Shaw admired it very much, he once again stormed about the little foyer of the Court Theatre when no one but the staff was about, complaining about the smallness of the houses and the financial results. For this he blamed the size of the theatre, the management, the production, the acting, the methods of publicity, the critics, and the play, especially if it were not his own; curiously enough, he never blamed the public. The public was never at fault and Shaw always wooed it, flattered it, scared it, insulted it, but never despised or was afraid of it. He now insisted that they try his play *The Philanderer*.

The Philanderer, always a play for which Shaw for some reason had great hopes, proved to be a greater disaster than *Captain Brassbound's Conversion*. Once again *You Never Can Tell*, which had always been a money-maker, saved the situation; but everyone connected with the Court seemed to realize that the time had come to take a larger theatre in the West End.

The Royal Court had made theatre history with an unprecedented total of thirty-two plays by seventeen authors. Actors had always been paid their salaries of at least three pounds a week. Vedrenne and Barker had both been paid twenty pounds a week and all of the authors had been paid their royalties. It is quite understandable, therefore, that by June, 1907, they closed their books with a slight debit. On a pretext, by refusing some of his royalties, Shaw was able to put them in the black.

The new Vedrenne-Barker Management rose like a phoenix from the ashes of the Court Theatre. They leased the Savoy from Mrs. D'Oyly Carte and this was the scene of their first West End venture, although later several other theatres were used, including a return to the Royal Court for occasional experimental matinees.

When the Vedrenne-Barker Management for the Savoy Theatre was formed, Shaw was asked to become a member of it, but he refused. "I am not going into partnership; I shall simply act as a usurer," he said. On these terms he put up the sum of 2,000 pounds at 5 percent interest to enable them to start, and Vedrenne and Barker put up 1,000 pounds each. Under their arrangement Vedrenne and Barker were each to continue to draw salaries of 1,000 pounds a year to be charged as expenses, with Barker receiving an additional salary as actor and fees as author when his plays were given. "My own salary, another thousand," said Shaw, "is to be taken out in moral superiority."

Theoretically all of the issues which the partners quarreled about at the Court should have been settled by the move to the Savoy. They were now near the heart of the theatre district where the bulk of London's theatre-going public expected to find their entertainment. The Savoy was a famous theatre and large enough, if business was good, to bring in the revenue needed for new plays as well as old.

Very shortly, however, trouble arose because of seriously divided opinions on many issues. The least of these was that Vedrenne was still opposed to Lillah playing so many leads. It was agreed she should only do so if the authors asked for her. Once again this was easy: Shaw always wanted her for his plays and sometimes even per-suaded her to appear in them against her better judgment.

A more serious matter was the fact that the great bonanza at the box office never materialized. C. B. Purdom, the careful chronicler of Barker's life, attributes this to the fact that the loyal supporters of the Court never felt at home at the Savoy. The audience of the Court was once described as not so much an audience as a congregation. Purdom might have added that many of them had already seen, perhaps several times, some of the Shaw successes that were to be repeated in the West End. But more importantly, the West End audiences were still not attracted by the "new" drama of Shaw and Galsworthy, or Barker's productions of Murray's Greek plays.

As a result Barker, always moody, became more and more depressed. Vedrenne became more and more concerned about his unbalanced budget. And Shaw was bitterly disappointed that the plays which had been acclaimed by the critics and public in the United States and on the continent, and even in England by the "congregation" of the Court, now were not finding favor in this invasion of the West End. Even the tried-and-true *You Never Can Tell* which was thought to be a play that could not fail to win them new friends failed to do so.

At the opening of the third bill, a revival of *The Devil's Disciple* with the popular leading man Matheson Lang as Dick Dudgeon, Shaw did what he was to do on several other occasions. He stayed away until the last few rehearsals, partly because he did not approve of the casting, partly because he thought Barker should not both produce and play General Burgoyne. Unfortunately, he was right. Barker's playing of the General, one of Shaw's greatest bits of writing, was brilliant, but Max Beerbohm slyly remarked in the *Saturday Review* that he felt that Barker's name on the program as producer was a printer's error:

> I find myself distracted between my sense of the facts that the production of *The Devil's Disciple* is a thoroughly bad one and my distaste of decrying anything done by Mr. Barker. . . . I am convinced that *The Devil's Disciple* was cast and stage managed by Mr. Vedrenne alone.[35]

Vedrenne was quite naturally furious and wanted to answer Beerbohm but Shaw persuaded him that it was just another of Max's little jokes.

The last play before the lease at the Savoy terminated was a revival of Shaw's *Arms and the Man* with Robert Loraine, a favorite actor of Shaw's, in the part of Bluntschli. It was also the nearest approach to a quarrel Shaw ever had with Lillah. She did not wish to play the part of Raina in the exaggerated and affected style that Shaw insisted upon. Consequently, as Shaw predicted, Loraine "acted her off the stage." Barker himself was not up to the flamboyant acting required for his role of Sergius, and the production as a whole was not favorably received.

The end was in sight for the Vedrenne-Barker Management. The shrewd little accountant was always, Shaw felt, a great balance for Barker, who never thought of such a mundane thing as money when he was involved in a play; perfection was more important than anything else although Shaw had been warning him of bankruptcy in letter after letter.

Actually the Vedrenne-Barker Management was not dissolved for several years, but when the books were closed it was heavily in debt. There was cash in the bank amounting to almost £500, but Shaw had during these years advanced over £5,000, so he accepted the cash with what other assets the management had and wrote the whole thing off. He had, in fact, made a profitable investment, as he well knew, since he had derived considerable royalties from the production of his plays. Vedrenne and Barker went their own separate ways and very shortly a new management was to take its place.

Shaw and Vedrenne now joined forces briefly with Frederick Harrison at the Haymarket, without Barker. Shaw's real objective was to have his new play *Getting Married* produced and to develop some semblance of a repertory. Barker had produced Masefield's *The Tragedy of Nan* for the actor's play-producing society, the Pioneer Players, at the Royalty on May 22. Shaw liked it and suggested to Vedrenne that they give three or four performances of it since Lillah was very good and the quality of the play was unmistakable. Shaw eventually had his way and the play had a number of matinees in spite of Vedrenne's opposition.

Shaw then began a campaign to get the Barkers to appear in *Getting Married*, but without success. In spite of his efforts to arouse public interest, sufficient support was not forthcoming, and the run ended and with it this coalition management. Shaw lost his personal investment, and it looked as if repertory theatre in London was doomed, although the following year help was to come from an unexpected source.

The Frohman Repertory and Lillah's Little Theatre

Despite the failure of the Vedrenne-Barker Management at the Savoy, talk of repertory theatres was being heard constantly in all London literary and theatrical circles. In April, 1909, Frederick Harrison and Herbert Trench announced a repertory season for the Haymarket. Granville Barker was discussed as a possible producer, but he had also been approached to form a repertory company at the Duke of York's Theatre under the aegis of the American manager Charles Frohman.

Frohman's interest in the Barkers had come about through a mutual friend and one-time neighbor, the playwright James Matthew Barrie. Frohman had made a fortune in producing Barrie plays both in England and in the United States where the actress Maude Adams created most of Barrie's leading roles. Now Barker persuaded Frohman that he should produce new plays not only by Barrie but also by Bernard Shaw, John Galsworthy, and himself in what was to become the first real repertory company in London. This meant that no play would be given for more than two or three performances consecutively but that each playwright should have several performances of his play each fortnight.

The first play produced was Galsworthy's *Justice*, directed by Barker, which opened February 1, 1910, to considerable critical acclaim. Even Barker's enemies granted that it was a brilliant production, and the play, dealing as it did with the inequities of the British penal code, immediately caused great excitement. Beatrice Webb was tremendously impressed and wrote in her diary that the play was "great in realistic form, great in its reserve and restraint, great in its quality of pity." Discussion of the play so interested young Winston Churchill, who at that time was Home Secretary, that he went to see it. He was so moved that he made a speech about it in the House of Commons which actually resulted in some reforms in the penal code.

Shaw's contribution to the Frohman project was *Misalliance*, which opened two nights later and did not receive as favorable a press as the Galsworthy play. Shaw had been dissatisfied with the actors since he had set his heart on the Barkers appearing in the leading roles. They did not, and *Misalliance* was utterly misunderstood by both audiences and critics although it has since proved to be one of Shaw's most popular plays. It was followed by a bill of one-act plays which also were not successful, although one of them was Barrie's famous *The Twelve Pound Look*, which was later to serve as a vehicle for so many great ladies of the theatre. Barker's new play *The Madras House* suffered a similar fate at the box office and at Frohman's insistence a revival of Pinero's *Trelawney of the Wells* was rushed into production, but to no avail, and on May 9, Shaw wrote to Barker: "The Shaw-Frohman combination is off," he declared. "His power stops at the commercial frontier . . . he is chucking the repertory altogether, as from now; also the devil (meaning you and me) and all his works."[36]

Frohman's venture was, while it lasted, a true repertory and proved that the system could be adapted to the London commercial theatre. Its failure was due, as Shaw had predicted, to a confusion of aims, and while it had not added to Shaw's reputation as a playwright, it had added considerably to the reputation of Barker as a director.

Barker, however, was very discouraged and was becoming more and more discontented with the London theatrical scene. He even talked of becoming a naturalized German citizen so he could produce plays in that country. It was because of this that Lillah McCarthy now conceived of another venture and quietly went about it in a woman's way. In the early months of 1911 the Barkers had taken a small flat over the newly-opened Little Theatre, Johns Street, Adelphi. It was indeed a little theatre since it seated only 278. Gertrude Kingston's original venture of the Laurence Housman translation of Aristophanes' *Lysistrata* had failed, and the theatre was now empty. Miss McCarthy, who was determined to keep Barker in England, went to Shaw and asked for a new play. "Get a theatre," he said, "and the play will be there—a money maker." Without saying anything further to Shaw or her husband, Lillah went off the following morning to Lord Howard De Walden and asked him for £1,000 to take the theatre and open it under the Barker-McCarthy Management. He gave her the £1,000, to which Shaw added £500 more and also the promise of *Fanny's First Play*. A few other friends contributed money and she took a lease of the Little Theatre. The Barkers were once again in management, this time one that was to be successful.

Lillah's Little Theatre was attractive, although rather precious, and the Barkers immediately set to work to make it more liveable and democratic in keeping with the traditions they had established at the Court and the Savoy. There were stalls for 250 and seven boxes at the back. Since there was no pit and therefore no seats at pit prices, they rather arbitrarily made the last two rows into pit seats at the old price of 2 shillings, 6 pence. They added a drama book stall in the attractive and spacious foyer. A. E. Drinkwater became the manager and remained with the McCarthy-Barker Management until the end.

The first plays produced were Schnitzler's *Anatol* and Ibsen's *The Master Builder*, in which Lillah McCarthy achieved the dream of a lifetime in the part of Hilda Wangel. Both were successful. Unfortunately Norman McKinnel, who played the title role in *The Master Builder*, had a previous commitment and the Barkers had to close the play while it was still playing to capacity audiences.

Lillah, now in great haste, appeared at the Shaw flat demanding the play he had promised her. Shaw was still rewriting *Fanny's First Play* but it was hurriedly staged with no more than a fortnight's rehearsal for an opening on

April 19. It was an instant and complete success and had the longest run of any Shaw play yet produced anywhere. This was partly because of Shaw's insistence that no author's name be attached to it. All of their friends started a word of mouth campaign in London theatrical circles assigning almost every playwright but Shaw to be the author. At first Shaw thought it best to produce it anonymously to avoid whatever disfavor his name might arouse with the critics. Later, however, he realized the publicity value of the curiosity which would be engendered by their little mystery.

Fanny's First Play is actually a play within a play. It begins with an induction scene in which Count O'Dowda, an Irish gentleman residing in Venice, has invited four prominent London critics to his country house to witness the presentation of a play written by his daughter Fanny. He explains to the impressario that the play (which he has not read) probably will be a dainty harlequinade. His daughter has been carefully sheltered and therefore would naturally not write a play dealing with the ugly realities of life from which she had been sheltered, except for the past two years when she had been in school at Cambridge. As a birthday present to her the most important London critics—Trotter, Vaughan, Gunn, and Flawner Bannel—have been invited.

After the prologue comes the play proper which is a hilarious satire on a respectable bourgeois family living in Denmark Hill who are concerned about the activities of their rebellious children, Bobby and Margaret. This involves continuous feuds and bickerings for the rest of the play, with the generation gap that existed at the run of the century dramatized brilliantly by Bernard Shaw.

In the epilogue Count O'Dowda is horrified by the play. The critics do not know what to make of it and there is a lively discussion as to who the author of the play might be, with Granville Barker's and Pinero's names suggested. When Flawner Bannel suggests that it might be Shaw, there is a heated discussion of that author's merits and demerits. At that point Fanny, in tears, tells them that she herself is the author of the play.

The tremendous success of this play prevented the Barkers from presenting anything like a repertory. It ran at the Little Theatre until the lease expired and revewal was refused. It was then transferred to a larger theatre, the Kingsway, where it continued to make money.

It was the first time that Shaw had allowed any of his plays to continue for a long run, since one of his crusades in the theatre had been to end the domination of the London commercial theatre with long-run plays. He became increasingly uneasy as the triumphant weeks went by and audiences that had rejected their attempts at repertory flocked to see *Fanny's First Play*. On its 200th performance he said to an interviewer:

> For the first time I have allowed a play of mine to run itself to death in the usual commercial fashion. . . . What reason have you to doubt that if I had allowed *John Bull's Other Island* or *You Never Can Tell* or *Man and Superman* to run on in the same way at the Court Theatre in the great days of Vedrenne and Barker, they would not have been running still?[37]

In the "great days of the Court Theatre" these three plays several times kept the creditors from the doors of the Court Theatre. They served the purpose of allowing the actors to return fresh to their parts after playing other roles. One drawback to this system of limited repertories, however, was that there were nearly always minor and sometimes major cast changes requiring more rehearsals.

Now with the end in view of establishing true repertory, with rotating plays by at least five authors, the Barkers leased the St. James Theatre. Their first production was Shaw's new play *Androcles and The Lion*, on September 1, 1913. Shaw was not present at any of the rehearsals, but he had admonished and instructed Barker by letter as to how this unusual play was to be presented. At dress rehearsal he arrived to find the playing too slow and restrained and he immediately took over. One of his biographers, Hesketh Pearson, who had a small part in the play, describes what happened: "He danced about the stage, spouting bits from all parts with folded arms . . . always exaggerating so as to

prevent our imitating him, making us all feel we were acting in a charade."³⁸ This was exactly Shaw's conception of
the play; a charade, or as he was later to describe it, an
adult Christmas pantomime complete with the imitation
lion. At 11:00 Shaw left the theatre telling Barker to pick up
the pieces.

In spite of this the play received fairly good reviews in
the daily papers and continued for fifty-two performances.
A storm of criticism followed, however, in many religious
periodicals, whose writers completely misunderstood
Shaw's intention. It was said that Shaw was ridiculing the
early Christian martyrs. In reality, he was simply saying
that the world was not yet ready for Christ's teachings, and
therefore Lavinia (Lillah McCarthy's part) and Ferrovius,
the gladiator, decide to relinquish martyrdom in order to
await the God that is to be. After the play was published
this was to be elaborated in one of the longest prefaces
which he had yet written.

The Barkers had lavished a great deal of time and
money on *Androcles* and it was the first Shaw play to be
given this treatment. By 1913 Barker had begun his scheme
for bringing creative artists into the theatre as stage
designers. Albert Rothenstein had been chosen to create the
decor for *Androcles* and it had received very favorable comment. Fifty-two performances was a respectable run in a
large theatre, and now the Barkers fulfilled a plan to continue at the St. James with three weeks of repertory, which
was to be the last real repertory of the McCarthy-Barker
Management in London. The playwrights included Ibsen,
Molière, Masefield, Galsworthy, and Shaw with his revival
The Doctor's Dilemma.

Barker addressed an appeal from the stage for further
support of a national repertory, but little money for that
was forthcoming, and the Barkers now turned to the
production of three plays by Shakespeare.

When Shakespeare was first mentioned to Shaw he was
utterly opposed, but gradually he warmed to the project.
Gordon Craig had just produced his *Hamlet* in Moscow
with the famous screen settings, and Shaw now thought
that perhaps the hour had come for a youthful Hamlet.

Shaw suggested to Barker that he try to get the entire Gordon Craig production, which had recently been a great success in Moscow, and play Hamlet himself. Perhaps, he added mischieviously, "Teddy would play the ghost of a lost soul," while Lillah "could make a new thing of the Queen."[39]

Instead of *Hamlet*, the plays selected by the Barkers were *A Winter's Tale, Twelfth Night,* and *A Midsummer Night's Dream.* The first of these set the tone for all three, and Barker now anticipated practically all subsequent Shakespeare productions in many ways. He broke out of the customary picture-frame settings by building another stage over the orchestra pit. This was not exactly Shakespeare's platform stage, of course, but it was something approximating it since it brought the actors closer to the audience. Now most of the action was on this large apron which was at a lower level than the permanent stage. This was used only in the manner of the inner stage of an Elizabethan theatre. The plays were given with one single interval of fifteen minutes. The speed of the production somewhat bewildered the audience, accustomed as they were to having Shakespeare pared down to a few memorable speeches performed in an elaborate and cavernous stage setting. Almost at once the intellectual journals of the day began saluting Barker as the new director who had at last revolutionized English staging.

In the intervening months before the declaration of war in August, 1914, the Barkers were busily engaged in raising funds for what might have become a national English repertory company. Many influential friends in the government were not only interested, but had even made investments. A trust fund was established, but with the war the money had to be returned to the contributors. Barker's work in the London theatre, save for a very few and relatively minor productions, was over.

V

Later Years
and Legacy

St. George and the Siren

Before the outbreak of the First World War both Shaw and
the Barkers had, perhaps, their greatest successes. Shaw at
long last had a major play *Pygmalion,* produced by one of
the greatest actor-managers of the day, Sir Herbert Beerbohm Tree, with Mrs. Pat Campbell as Eliza Doolittle, and
the Barkers three plays of Shakespeare are still landmarks in
the history of Shakespearean stagecraft. But on these ventures they worked independently of one another—a
forecast of the dissolution of their partnership.

Until 1912, when he first read *Pygmalion* to her, Shaw
had had few personal encounters with Mrs. Pat Campbell.
While he and Barker were beginning the Court Theatre
venture, Mrs. Pat was touring the United States on no less
than three different occasions. But she did eventually play
Ibsen's *Hedda Gabbler* at the Court Theatre for a week of
matinees. In her memoirs she recalls "that Mr. Barker
attended the rehearsals and sometimes Mr. Bernard Shaw;
their 'basso relievo' methods fidgeted me. However, as far
as I remember they left me alone."[1] Mrs. Campbell was
rather successful as Hedda and even volunteered to play it
in an extended evening engagement. Vedrenne, however,
still licking the financial wounds caused by bringing in
Ellen Terry as a star, declined her offer. Instead Mrs. Pat

117

toured the provinces in the play under her own management. Now, after almost fifteen years, Shaw returned to a
project which he had begun as early as 1897.

In a letter to Ellen Terry at that time, Shaw told her:
"*Caesar and Cleopatra* has been driven clean out of my
mind by a play I want to write for them (Forbes-Robertson
and Mrs. Campbell) in which he shall be a West End
gentleman and she an East End dona in an apron and three
orange and red ostrich feathers."[2]

Now, over a decade later he completed *Pygmalion* and
arranged to read it one evening to Dame Edith Lyttleton;
he also arranged that Mrs. Campbell, a close friend of hers,
should be there. This, too, he describes to Ellen:

> I now have a grotesque confession to make to you. I wrote
> a play for Alexander which was really a play for Mrs. Patrick
> Campbell. It is almost as wonderful a fit as Brassbound; for I
> am a good ladies' tailor, whatever my shortcomings may be.
> And the part is SO different, not a bit in the world like Lady
> Cicely. ("I should think not" you will say.) Then came the
> Question, would *she* stand it? For, I repeat, this heroine
> wasn't a Lady Cicely Wayneflete: she was Liza Doolittle, a
> flower girl, using awful language and wearing an apron and
> three ostrich feathers, and having her hat put in the oven to
> slay the creepy-crawlies, and being taken off the stage and
> washed, like Drinkwater. I simply didn't dare offer it to her.
> Well, I read it to a good friend of mine, and contrived that
> she should be there. And she *was* there, reeking from *Bella
> Donna*. She saw through it like a shot. "You beast, you wrote
> this for me, every line of it: I can hear you mimicking my
> voice in it, etc. etc." And she rose to the occasion, quite fine
> and dignified for a necessary moment, and said unaffectedly
> she was flattered. And then—and then—oh Ellen; and then?
> Why then I went calmly to her house to discuss business
> with her, as hard as nails, and, as I am a living man, fell head
> over ears in love with her in thirty seconds. And it lasted
> more than thirty hours. I made no struggle: I went in head
> over ears, and dreamed and dreamed and walked on air for
> all that afternoon and the next day as if my next birthday
> were my twentieth. And I said, among other things (to
> myself) "Now I shall amuse and interest Ellen again for at
> least one letter or two." Which I am accordingly trying to
> do.[3]

Ellen's reply, as always, was sincere but somewhat guarded:

> It was a joy to get your letter, *I'm* in love with Mrs. Campbell too, or rather I'd like to be, but something tugs me back. She is amusing and was nice to me in America. The flower-girl idea is thrilling.[4]

Unfortunately Shaw did not accept her implied warning but plunged recklessly ahead. In the preceding fifteen years of his married life he had had no important romantic attachments with the actresses with whom he was involved, but now everyone was told of this one. Mrs. Campbell received almost daily letters and there were frequent meetings. He writes to her:

> Many thanks for Friday, and for a Saturday of delightful dreams. I did not believe that I had that left in me. I am all right now, down on earth again with all my cymbals and side drums and glaring vulgarities in full blast; but it would be meanly cowardly to pretend that you are not a very wonderful lady, or that the spell did not work most enchantingly on me for fully 12 hours.[5]

Shaw's letters were still a careful blend of business and paper passion. In a letter dated July 3, although he addresses her "Beatrissima" he is trying to persuade her that *Pygmalion* would not have a chance for success if she produced it with herself as a star:

> O Stella Stellarum, there is nothing more certain in the suns than if you attempt management on the single star system. Nothing—not even my genius added to your own—can save you from final defeat . . . . Your public is more than half feminine: you cannot satisfy their longing for a male to idealize; and how can they idealize a poor salaried employee pushed into a corner and played off the stage?[6]

They continued to disagree for some time about a choice of leading men, Shaw holding out for Robert Loraine, who had made a great success of *Man and Superman* both in New York and London. Mrs. Campbell, however, said that if Shaw preferred Loraine as an actor-manager to herself as an actress-manager, he could produce the play in the United States or anywhere else with whatever actress he pleased as Eliza.

Shaw then changed his approach and went further into his filing box of actors for a leading man. Whenever he came up with a suggestion, however, Mrs. Campbell would counter with another. Some of these were almost unbelievable. One of her choices was none other than James Carew, Ellen Terry's former husband, who had been elevated to the role of Captain Brassbound during Ellen's American tour. This and other suggestions by Mrs. Campbell indicate how little she understood the part of Henry Higgins.

This was the state of their negotiations for the production of *Pygmalion* when Mrs. Campbell was involved in a serious taxi accident. At first the extent of her injuries were not fully realized, and an understudy went on for her in Robert Hichen's melodrama *Bella Donna*, in which she was then appearing. Two weeks later her physician advised her that it would be months before she could return to the part and she left England with Sir Edward and Lady Stracey to recuperate in the south of France.

After her return to England their relationship, however, still confined itself mostly to business:

> I could not love thee, dear, so much, loved I not money more. . . . I must go now and read this to Charlotte. My love affairs are her unfailing amusement: all their tenderness recoils finally on herself.[7]

But in May, 1913, Shaw had purchased a motorcycle so that he could go off for meetings with Mrs. Campbell without using the family Rolls Royce. About this time Charlotte accidentally overheard a telephone conversation between Shaw and Mrs. Pat which deeply disturbed her. Shaw tells Mrs. Pat that the effect was dreadful:

> It hurts me miserably to see anyone suffer like that. I must, it seems, murder myself or else murder her. . . . Well, I daresay it's good for us all to suffer; but it's hard that the weak should suffer the most. If I could be human and suffer with a suffering of my own there would be some poetic justice in it; but I can't: I can only feel the sufferings of others with a paint that pity makes, and with a fierce im-

patience of it—the essential inhumanity of this jealousy that
I never seem able to escape from.[8]

There was no doubting the fact that now Charlotte was
jealous, but this did not prevent Shaw and Mrs. Pat from
meeting in secret at his sister Lucy's house at Denmark
Hill. Lucy, no doubt, enjoyed this tremendously since she
had never liked Charlotte and she now became a close
friend of Mrs. Pat. Complications soon arose, however,
because Mrs. Pat was receiving the addresses of George
Cornwallis-West, a distinguished gentleman who would
shortly become a lord. Early in August she left London for
the Guildford Hotel at Sandwich. Her intention apparently
was to escape her importunate fifty-seven-year-old lover,
whose plans did not include matrimony. But Shaw was now
for the last time in his life an almost obsessed man. He
followed her there although she refused to see him and sent
him this note:

> Please will you go back to London today—or go wherever
> you like but don't stay here—if you won't go I must—I am
> very very tired and I oughtn't to go another journey. Please
> don't make me despise you.   *Stella.*[9]

Shaw would not take this for an answer, for it seemed
to him the mystic moment when their geniuses should be
united and their love consummated. Mrs. Pat, now
realizing that her impending marriage was in danger, and
seeing the serious complications of what would happen if
she became his mistress, left him a brief note and fled.
Shaw's rage and frustrated fury knew no bounds. His next
two letters contained the most magnificent fulminations
against Mrs. Pat Campbell and all womanhood that have
ever been penned:

> Very well, go. The loss of a woman is not the end of the
> world. The sun shines; it is pleasant to swim; it is good to
> work; my soul can stand alone. But I am deeply, deeply,
> deeply wounded. . . .[10]

The next day he wrote again in the same vein:

> Oh my rancor is not slaked: I have not said enough vile
> things to you . . . I almost condescended to romance. I
> risked the breaking of deep roots and sanctified ties; I set my

feet boldly on all the quicksands: I rushed after Will o' the Wisp into darkness: I courted the oldest illusions, knowing well what I was doing. I seized handfuls of withered leaves and said, "I accept them for gold." [11]

More bitter recriminations were to follow, but Shaw eventually returned to Ayot St. Lawrence. He took Charlotte for a motoring trip on the continent and they were reconciled:

> . . . after two perfectly frightful scenes with me, in which she produced such a case against my career and character as made Bluebeard seem an angel in comparison, she quite suddenly and miraculously—at a moment when murder and suicide seemed the only thing left to her—recovered her intellectual balance, her sanity, and her amiability completely, and became once again (after about two years) the happy consort of an easygoing man. . . . [12]

Early in 1914 plans were finally completed for Sir Herbert Beerbohm Tree to play Henry Higgins opposite Mrs. Pat at His Majesty's Theatre. Shaw was to direct it and wrote a New Year's Eve letter to Mrs. Pat romantically recalling the previous New Year's Eve they had spent together when she, always the coquette, had persuaded him to stay with her instead of going on to a party with Barrie and Lillah McCarthy.

Rehearsals for the play began in friendly enough fashion. Apparently Shaw as director functioned in his usual manner: the actors were given their blocking, script in hand, and this went on for the usual week. There is one almost humble letter from Mrs. Pat asking his approval for a change in a scene with which she was having difficulties. The new blocking had met with the approval of Sir Herbert and the other members of the cast and she is now asking for Shaw's permission to play it the new way. Another letter invited him for supper at 5:30 in order to go over her part.

When they went into the last two weeks of rehearsal, however, Shaw found that he was dealing with not one but two veteran actors who were not accustomed to the meticulous attention to detail which he had given the players at the Court Theatre. Both for years had been stars in their own right and were used to performing in their own way without any interference from an author-director. Both of them began receiving the usual notes about their pronunciation and interpretation of their roles. None of these seem to have survived; probably Mrs. Pat tore hers up, for her replies indicate increasing bitterness at Shaw's interference. He had at one point nailed some properties to a table to keep her in the playing positions assigned.

Probably Shaw's disposition was not helped when he learned, on April 6, five days before the opening of the play, of Mrs. Pat's marriage to George Cornwallis-West. By that time the stage of His Majesty's Theatre resembled a battlefield and Mrs. Pat was finally to announce in her best prima donna fashion that either Mr. Shaw would leave the theatre or she would. Shaw left the theatre. Thereafter he was told he could communicate with her only through the stage manager. Of course Shaw did no such thing and on the day of the opening wrote a letter headed:

FINAL ORDERS.

> . . . The danger tonight will be a collapse of the play after the third act. I am sending a letter to Tree which will pull him together if it does not kill him. But a good deal will depend on whether you are inspired at the last moment. You are not, like me, a great general. You leave everything to chance, whereas Napoleon and Caesar left nothing to chance except the last inch that is in the hands of destiny. I could have planned the part so that nine tenths of it would have gone mechanically even if your genius had deserted you, leaving only one tenth to the Gods. Even as it is, I have forced half the battle on you; but winning half the battle will not avert defeat. You believe in courage: I say "God save me from having to fall back on that desperate resource," though if it must come to that it must. I don't like fighting: I like conquering. You think you like fighting; and now you will have to succeed sword in hand. You have left yourself poorly provided with ideas and expedients; and you must make up for them by dash and brilliancy and resolution. And so, *Avanti!*[13]

Mrs. Pat's reply was almost in the nature of an apology:

Dear Joey,
   All success to you to-night.
   It's nice to think of your friendship and your genius—I'll
obey orders faithfully, I am so thankful you carried through
your giant's work to the finish—

Stella.[14]

In spite of all premonitions of failure the opening was
something of a triumph. One of the few problems seemed
to have been that in the scene at Mrs. Higgins' at-home
day, when Eliza is taken to try out her improved diction,
some of the lines could not be heard. Eliza has been told to
speak only about the weather after polite inquiries about
the guests' health. Carried away with her success she
described the death of her aunt from influenza so vividly
that Higgins and Pickering hasten her departure. What
made the play something of a *succès de scandale* were
Eliza's parting remarks which were distinctly heard:

> *Liza.* (nodding to the others). Goodbye, all.
> *Freddy.* (opening the door for her). Are you walking
> across the park, Miss Doolittle? If so—
> *Liza.* Walk! Not bloody likely. (Sensation). I am going in
> a taxi. (She goes out.)[15]

It was the first time that such an expression had ever
been heard in a West End Theatre. Tree was even asked by
the Managers' Association to remove it from the play, and it
is to his credit that he stood his ground and kept it in. He
was motivated, no doubt, partly by the fact that the publicity value was helping to fill his theatre with capacity
audiences at almost every performance. But he might also
have been motivated by the fact that it would be one less
quarrel with Shaw over what was happening to the play.
   Six days after the opening Mrs. Pat wrote that she had
a thousand things to tell him and to come see the play soon
or he would not recognize it. This was, perhaps, to place the
blame on Sir Herbert for the new ending which they had
devised for the play. Shaw had intended Eliza to exit in
defiance at the final curtain. Now Sir Herbert was gallantly
tossing her a bouquet of roses as the curtain was descend-
ing.

When Shaw published the play he added a long postscript giving his reasons why Eliza would never return to Wimpole Street to live with Higgins and Pickering "like three jolly bachelors," but would marry Freddy and get Colonel Pickering to loan them money to open a shop. What London saw, however, was Tree's version. Many years later when the film version with Wendy Hiller and Leslie Howard was made, Shaw permitted the film to end with a reconciliation. In 1914 Shaw was a bitter man, however, and resented the fact that Tree had turned the play into a romantic comedy with a cockney Cinderella who was to melt the hard heart of a professor of phonetics.

It seems ironic that Shaw's first great West End success in a major commercial theatre, with a probable run of many hundreds of performances, should have been cut short by the outbreak of World War I in August. Almost immediately after the assassination of the Archduke of Austria at Sarajevo, Sir Herbert posted a closing notice in spite of the fact that the play had drawn £2,000 that week. Mrs. Pat wrote Shaw frantically asking for his intervention and, if that failed, permission to take Sir George Alexander's St. James Theatre with the cast she wanted to take with her to America. The play closed, however, after 118 performances, but Mrs. Pat did take the play to America under the management of George C. Tyler, with Philip Merivale, who had made such a success of the role of Colonel Pickering, now playing Higgins.

Shaw tried his best to see to it that in America Mrs. Pat should do *his* play and not Beerbohm Tree's version of it. When Tyler wrote Shaw telling him that Mrs. Campbell had requested that a half-hour playing time be cut from the script for her New York appearance, he answered that it was Mrs. Campbell's changes of costume that would take longer than the changes of scenery. Tyler was advised to arrange dressing-room accommodations to avoid any running up and down stairs. "If you cannot give her a room on the stage level she will agitate for a tent (she had one at His Majesty's here); and when she starts agitating don't argue but surrender at once, even if it involves rebuilding the theatre. You will find it cheaper in the long run." He advised the strategy of agreeing with her in everything and told Tyler to blame the fact that the play had to be presented without cuts on Shaw's own "pigheadedness."

> It's no use arguing; she's clever enough to talk your hair grey; but she has no more judgement than a baby, and will spoil the play if you let her. She doesn't know where the interest of the play really comes; and does not care twopence about the part, to which she has never given five minutes to serious thought . . . the moral of all this is that for her sake and for your own you must stick to me and to the play, and resist all her wiles to have it cut down . . . if mortal man can resist such a siren, which I rather doubt.[16]

He was justified in being anxious about what Mrs. Pat would do to *Pygmalion* without his presence as scourge and mentor. In America, no doubt, in the last act the bouquet of roses would be tossed to her and any other additions made that suited the whim of the moment. Some time later when playing Eliza in 1920 for Viola Tree at the Aldwych Theatre, she "lost" her prompt book of the American tour. Shaw immediately accused her of losing it on purpose:

> You think I should be shocked by all the cuts and gags. Nonsense! Trot it out: I shant be surprised.[17]

This was to be Mrs. Pat's last Eliza. As a veteran of hundreds of performances she was excused from many of the rehearsals nor did Shaw himself attend many of them. When he finally did see it he wrote to her a summation of all his criticism during the ten years they had worked on the play:

> Belovedest
>   I was in front last night. You have now got the play as nearly as you like it as you will ever get it. . . .
>   You now play the second act (the first part) and the fifth act so very cleverly and nicely that I damned you up hill and down dale for doing it so badly for me when you could do it so well for yourself. It is now really good Victorian drawing room drama, pleasant and sweet, and in what you (bless you!) call good taste. You are not a great actress in a big play or anything disturbing or vulgar of that sort; but you have your hearts desire, and are very charming. Kate Rorke at her

best could not have improved on it. I enjoyed it and appreciated it in its little way. And that was magnanimous of me, considering how I missed the big bones of my play, its fortissimos, its allegros, its precipitous moments, its contrasts, and all its big bits. My orchestration was feeble on the cottage piano; and my cymbals were rather disappointing on the cups and saucers. Still, you were happy; and that was something. And Higgins was not brutal to you, as I was.[18]

Shortly after her return to England from America at the death of her father-in-law, Mrs. Pat became Lady Beatrice Cornwallis-West and mistress of Ruthin Castle in North Wales. The adjustment to the loss of his "Stella Stellarum" to another was not an easy one for Shaw. Sheer senility, the Webbs called his infatuation, but obsession might be the better word. Years later, Alexander Woolcott described a luncheon with the Shaws at his villa in the south of France when Shaw talked about Mrs. Pat at such length that Mrs. Shaw began drumming on the table with her fork to silence him. Shaw probably was not silenced, but at least the subject was changed.

They continued to correspond as long as Mrs. Pat lived, since toward the end of her life they had something more to quarrel about. Mrs. Pat, now in serious financial difficulties, wanted to publish their letters in *Mrs. Pat Campbell: My Life and Some Letters*. Shaw had allowed her to use a few in the volume published in 1922, but he refused to permit any further publication until after Charlotte's death. She also wanted him to send her money so that she might return to England. He tells her candidly and brutally:

> . . . If only you could write a true book, entitled, *Why, Though I Was a Wonderful Actress, No Manager or Author Would Ever Engage Me Twice If He Could Possibly Help It*, it would be a best seller. . . . As to bringing you over. I had as soon bring the devil over. You would upset me and everybody else.[19]

Mrs. Pat indignantly replied with a list of the actor-managers who had engaged her:

This last letter of yours is full of craziness, and unbelievable unkindness:
     "No Manager would engage you a second time if he could
help it."
     Six engagements with Alexander—counting two
revivals—and please remember I gave in my notice. . . .
Nine engagements with Robertson—until Hamlet and his
pretty wife left no place for me.
Four plays with Gerald du Maurier. . . . *Two* with Hare,
Four with Tree . . . but what's the use of bothering about
your willful nonsense, and by now I daresay you have
forgotten all you wrote in this last letter!
     And you dare to accuse me of humiliating people! Since
you first dipped your pen in the ink-pot what else have you
ever done?[20]

Her last years were, as most of her life had been, sad;
and at the same time richly comic. Alexander Woolcott
described her as a sinking ship firing on all who tried to
help her. Shaw did send her money and offered her small
parts in the film versions of *Pygmalion* and *Major Barbara*
but Mrs. Pat was difficult to the last.

Perhaps the truth about Mrs. Pat's being "difficult" is
simply that she became bored with long runs and gave
careless, indifferent performances, relying as she could on
her charm to give the customers satisfaction. When she was
in a play that challenged her, as when she played *Hedda
Gabbler* in matinees at the Court Theatre, she was "charm
itself." She cooperated with the other members of the company and was guilty of none of the displays of temper that
marked her career when she was appearing in her long-run
performances in the West End Theatre.

Her "glorious voice" was to follow Shaw for many
years—even after he thought he had forgotten her. In his
Heartbreak House she was the seductress Hesione
Hushabye. Nor was this the only time that Shaw was to put
Mrs. Pat into a play. In his masterpiece *Back to Methuselah*
Shaw says the serpent in the Garden of Eden always spoke
to him with her voice. She was also, he claimed, Orinthia in
The Apple Cart. In this play when King Magnus wishes
dutifully to return to his wife, his mistress Orinthia tries for-

cibly to detain him and the two are wrestling about on the floor when they are interrupted by a servant. Shaw maintains that this actually happened on one occasion when he wished to return to Charlotte, but Mrs. Pat perversely wanted him to stay with her. Mrs. Pat objected strongly to this wrestling scene in *The Apple Cart* and called it "mischievous vulgarity and untruthfulness."[21] Probably it wasn't, for whatever their relationship was it was not platonic, and the play may have been written as a last attempt to appease Charlotte.

If Shaw's relationship with Janet Achurch and Charles Charrington resulted in one bad novel, his romance with Mrs. Pat Campbell resulted in two bad plays. The first of these, *Dear Liar* by Jerome Kilty, was more of a lecture-recital of the Shaw-Campbell letters. It was Katherine Cornell's last production, with Brian Aherne playing the Shaw part, and they read the letters from lecterns with a few scenes from the plays dramatized. What distinguished this production was Brian Aherne's performance as Bernard Shaw for the simple reason that he had all the best lines. These love letters of Shaw's are sometimes Shaw at his epistolary best. Unfortunately Miss Cornell as Mrs. Pat Campbell, although very beautiful and magnificently gowned, was in no way able to suggest the personality of the tempestuous Mrs. Campbell.

The second play dramatizing the Shaw-Campbell romance is *A Fig Leaf In Her Bonnet* by Jesse Torn. It had a short run at the Gramercy Arts Theatre in New York in June of 1961. The author describes its reception:

> The critical reaction was sharply divided, apparently on the horary basis, for the PM newspaper reviewers praised the play while the AM critics were incredulous and even shocked at the notion that Shaw had been emotionally involved with Mrs. Campbell. The corporate image of Shaw as the gay anchorite above the sordid commonplaces of sex, love and humanity had been violated.[22]

Readers of the Shaw biographies, particularly that of St. John Ervine, should hardly have been shocked. What distinguishes this play from the biographical accounts is

that it is written from Mrs. Campbell's point of view. Shaw
comes off rather badly for the heartless way in which he
treated both Charlotte and Stella. According to Jesse Torn,
Stella actually wrote him a love letter leaving the way
squarely open for a marriage proposal:

> His characteristic response was to recoil in terror and flight.
> Mrs. Campbell then had a very serious setback in her health,
> a circumstance unconnected to this rejection. But she came
> back—Mrs. Campbell was nothing if not a fighter—and
> went after him with all the guile and determination of a
> widow.[23]

The play then records the meetings at Shaw's sister's, the
fatal assignation at Sandwich from which Mrs. Campbell
fled, and a last scene during the stormy rehearsals of
Pygmalion on the stage of the Royalty Theatre. Mrs.
Campbell there reveals to Shaw that she had married
George Cornwallis-West that afternoon.

Mrs. Torn's version of their last rehearsal meeting is of
Mrs. Campbell triumphant while her Joey, the clown at
that moment, takes off his greasepaint and putty-nose for
the last time. It is not this, however, that revolted the ar-
dent Shavians, but the fact that the dialogue is false and
weak. Mrs. Torn makes no attempt to use any of the letters
and in this she was right, since they probably could not be
fitted in. But the dialogue which she does put in the mouths
of her characters in no way suggests either Shaw or Mrs.
Campbell.

The End of a Partnership

The Barker Shakespeare productions did not have to be
closed because of the outbreak of hostilities in 1914 as did
Shaw's *Pygmalion*, but they did put an end to the Barker-
Shaw dream of a national theatre in England. Late in 1914
Barker's theatrical interests were transferred to New York
City where he had been invited by the Stage Society of
New York to do a series of productions. He was offered the
sum of $25,000 and was told he could choose his own com-
pany. Naturally he wished to include Lillah McCarthy, but

she was at the time the leading lady at the Haymarket Theatre and received the suggestion without enthusiasm. Both Shaw and Barrie, however, advised her to go for Barker's sake and so she consented to join the company on the New York venture.[24]

Whether or not Barker met Helen Huntington at this time is not known. At the conclusion of the New York engagement the company returned to England, but Barker joined the Red Cross and was sent back to the United States to lecture. Not long afterward both Lillah and Shaw received letters in the same mail telling them that he wanted a divorce. Lillah McCarthy went at once to Shaw and describes their meeting in a letter omitted from her memoirs:

> . . . Shaw greeted me very tenderly and made me sit by the fire. I was shivering. Shaw sat very still. The fire brought me warmth. . . . How long we sat there I do not know, but presently I found myself walking with dragging steps with Shaw beside me . . . up and down Adelphi Terrace. The weight upon me grew a little lighter and released the tears which would never come before . . . he let me cry. Presently I heard a voice in which all the gentleness and tenderness of the world was speaking. It said: "Look up, dear, look up to the heavens. There is more in life than this. There is much more."[25]

In spite of this consolation, Lillah McCarthy could not bring herself to believe that such a partnership as theirs could be terminated so summarily. Shaw, moreover, was besieged by letters from Barker to convince his wife that his mind was irrevocably made up. Shaw was in the unenviable position of being unable to satisfy either of his friends in the matter and his long correspondence with Barker was a very unhappy one. Instead of planning constructively for performances of plays which were to be one of the most distinguished chapters in the history of the English theatre, Shaw was now acting as a go-between in the dissolution of a great partnership. Eventually Lillah McCarthy, convinced that Barker would never return to her, divorced him. Helen Huntington had, meanwhile, divorced her husband and

was given a magnificent settlement. She and Barker were
married in London on July 13, 1918. Shaw continued to be
a friend of Lillah McCarthy for many years, but it was an
end to his relationship with Barker except for brief
meetings. As a wealthy American poetess, Helen Barker disliked socialists, pacifists, actors, and playwrights. Barker,
therefore, did very little more in the theatre and now
entered into a new career as a Shakespeare critic. This his
wife seemed to find acceptable. The last time Shaw saw
Barker was when he came to Ayot St. Lawrence to beg
Shaw not to write a preface to Lillah McCarthy's memoirs.
This Shaw refused to do and Barker left in anger only to
return moments later to say "we can't part like this." Barker
finally allowed his former wife to publish her volume
Myself and Some of My Friends only if his name were not
mentioned. This meant that the account of the plays in
which the Barkers appeared at the Court is severely ab-
breviated. Shaw, too, does not mention Barker's name in
the introduction to this book which might have been one of
the most interesting accounts of the Court Theatre if it had
not been butchered to please Helen Barker.

Brooks Atkinson calls Barker's estrangement from
Shaw "cowardly." It was certainly a serious mistake for
Barker to forego the rich companionship of a brilliant
playwright and his own career as England's most important
director. Such was his decision, however, and his
biographer C. B. Purdom feels that the last years of Barker's
life were more than tinged with sadness:

> From the point of view from which I am writing, to say that
> a man's life is tragedy is to acknowledge greatness, for it is to
> speak of him in relation to spiritual values, in which sphere
> tragedy lies. . . . That is how I see the life of Granville
> Barker and why I think his life important. I do not say the
> tragedy is clear, but it is certain, and to contemplate it is
> highly worthwhile and will occupy much attention in time
> to come.[26]

Many years later, after Charlotte's death, in his first
sense of loss and loneliness, Granville Barker was one of the
first people with whom Shaw wished to communicate. He

wrote him a pathetic postcard which concluded their correspondence:

> Charlotte died last Sunday, the 12th of September, at half past two in the morning. She had not forgotten you.
>
> Since 1939 she has suffered much pain and lately some distress from hallucinations of crowds of people in her room; and the disease, a horror called osteitis deformans which bent and furrowed her into a Macbeth witch (an amiable one), was progressing steadily and incurably. But last Friday a miracle occurred. She suddenly threw off her years, her visions, her furrows, her distresses, and had thirty hours of youth and happiness before the little breath she could draw failed. By morning she looked twenty years younger than you or I ever knew her.
>
> It was a blessedly happy ending; but you could not have believed that I should be as deeply moved. You will not, I know, mind my writing this to you. She was 86. I am 87.[27]

Barker did reply to this card but the letter has not survived. He, himself, died in Paris three years later at the age of sixty-eight.

Shaw and Barker: Their Achievement

Many times when the art of the theatre was such that a great dramatic literature was produced it was because the playwright was closely associated with an acting group (and often a great director) that produced his plays. O'Neill worked closely with those dedicated artists at the Provincetown Theatre and Theatre Guild. Chekhov might have never written his last plays if Stanislavski hadn't begun producing them. And Shaw was perhaps at his most creative when working with Granville Barker. The Court Players not only proved that the plays that Shaw had already written could be done, but the very existence of such a company kept him at the colossal task of writing six more major plays for them.

This did not mean that there were not serious disagreements between Shaw and Barker in mounting the plays. Shaw had a gift for Irish invective and never believed in understating his case. When Barker was casting *Major Barbara* he suggested Edmund Gwenn for Snobby Price:

> The difficulty about Snobby is that you have simply no sense of character. . . . Of course Gwenn can play a thief. He can also play the Emperor of China. An actor is an actor and a part is only a part when all's said. . .[28]

To tell a director that he has no sense of character is really hitting him where it hurts, which is just what Shaw intended to do, and he did it again and again.

Poor Barker was given another tongue-lashing when Shaw discovered that *The Devil's Disciple* was in difficulty at the Savoy. Shaw was vacationing in Wales and Barker alone was producing the play for the first time:

> Dear Barker,
>   I knew you wouldn't be able to stage-manage D's D. The business is all in the book: it worked so perfectly at the rehearsal that Robertson said "Oh, this is an easy play." The doors are like this. . . .[29]

Accompanying the letter are detailed floor plans for all three acts of the play.

Nothing could better indicate the closeness of the two men than a letter a month later, this time when *You Never Can Tell* was in trouble:

> . . . I should have come up for the last few rehearsals: the combination works better than the single cylinder. You are so afraid of their acting badly that you make them afraid too. And you exhaust yourself over the job until you have no oxygen to turn on at the end. However, a bit of training does them no harm, it will enable me to let them rip all the more recklessly next time.[30]

This clearly indicates the way in which they worked together. Barker, the veteran actor-director worked closely with the cast—Shaw thought sometimes too closely—although he admitted that this helped train the company as a whole. Shaw would come in at final rehearsals to pull the production together and to produce recklessly the bravura and overall effect he wanted for his plays.

Shaw leveled much the same criticisms at Barker as an actor as he did at Barker the director. He particularly disliked his "irritating habit of lowering his voice when he should have raised it." Nevertheless, he always wanted

Barker for his plays, because he possessed one invaluable asset: even if he sometimes wanted to underplay his own part, he had the ability that some rare actors have of pulling the whole production along with him. His intensity and understanding of the play was communicated to everyone in the cast.

Many of the critics of the theatre would agree with Shaw that, as an actor, Barker had serious deficiencies. His expression was inclined to be set with no remarkable play of feature except for his eyes which were very expressive. On these he relied for the impression he wished to create. His voice was light and one unkind critic described it as adenoidal. C. B. Purdom, his biographer, who saw him perform many times, always felt rather that it should be called "high pitched with excited ecstatic qualities containing little depth or fullness, but musical and altogether distinctive."[31] His gestures were spare, his hands delicate, and his fingers sensitive. If his posture was somewhat stiff, his movements were quick, never extravagant, and always elegant. This was probably why he made such an impression on Shaw when he first saw him as Marchbanks in *Candida*, a part which he had despaired of casting properly.

St. John Ervine, who also knew Barker well, disliked both the man, his acting, and his plays and constantly uses the word "dreary" to describe them all. He did admire some of his productions, however. Like many directors, Ervine felt that Barker, although himself a monotonous actor, was able to tell other people how to act. His mastery over insignificant detail was such that when the details were added together they amounted to revelation. Ervine recalls in particular Barker's direction in the courtroom scene of Galsworthy's *Justice:*

> . . . During Falder's trial, immense effect was obtained by the lighting of lamps as the evening closed on the final episodes of the trial. The lights, one after another at intervals were turned on; and the accumulated result of this illumination was strong enough to be vividly remembered by one enthralled spectator forty-five years after it was witnessed.[32]

Ervine also recalls that Barker's production of *Twelfth Night* was the most beautiful he had ever seen on any stage. This indeed is great praise, since Ervine as a dramatic critic had seen almost every major production in the English theatre over a considerable period of years.

In the staging of the plays, the building of scenery, and the lighting, Barker knew a great deal more about the practicalities of what was possible on the little Court stage than did Shaw. In reading through the letters it becomes fairly obvious that Shaw, in these categories, was at first relatively unimaginative. Of course with only a £200 budget for each play, the properties, furniture, and flats probably had to be used again and again. At this time stage design in some of the best theatres consisted simply of the director giving a floor plan to a stage carpenter.

Later on, after Barker and Vedrenne were planning on leaving the Court for a larger theatre in the West End, we find Shaw's letters to Barker suggesting more complicated stage settings and designs. Although always critical of Gordon Craig as impractical and lazy, both Shaw and Barker began thinking in terms of the innovations which they had seen him using, particularly in his productions of Ibsen's *The Vikings* and Shakespeare's *Much Ado About Nothing* for his mother, Ellen Terry.

When Florence Farr wrote to Shaw asking him if she might produce *Don Juan in Hell*, he wrote back telling her that of course it must be done in the Gordon Craig manner, with overhead lighting and the footlights abolished. Barker also in his later productions began using spotlights installed in the balcony to light the stage. And in his last productions, artists who were trained draughtsmen were hired to design the entire production including, sometimes, the costumes.

One of the things that most distinguished Shaw from Barker was his attitude toward the members of the company. Barker really never liked actors. His close friends were always authors (like Masefield and Galsworthy) and scholars (like William Archer and Gilbert Murray). As the Barkers' fame grew, they became intimate with many men and women prominent in government and society.

Shaw on the other hand, although always maintaining

close ties with Fabian friends (many of whom were now moving up in government circles) always remained in touch with everyone he knew in the theatre and corresponded with many of them, showering them with advice of all kinds, both professional and unprofessional. Some of them were surreptitiously aided financially and many of them made frequent pilgrimages to Ayot St. Lawrence, and all of them treasured his letters.

The War Years

The war years changed the lives of everyone in England, and Bernard Shaw was no exception. From the first hostilities, he was a conscientious objector, as were many of his fellow Fabians, but few were as vocal as he in proclaiming that England as well as Germany was an aggressor. One article in particular entitled "Common Sense About The War" brought down a storm of wrath upon him and alienated many old friends. Some of them, including the playwright Henry Arthur Jones, were never to be reconciled to him for his insistence that the war guilt was a collective guilt.

From 1914 to 1920 Shaw wrote only one major play *Heartbreak House;* all the others were one-act plays and most of these were produced for only a few performances. At this time there were few Shaw revivals and these only in the provinces. Shaw's life changed in many other ways. During the early years of the war, Florence Farr and Janet Achurch died within a year of one another. The Barkers were divorced. Many other old ties were broken. Shaw did, however, continue to see many of his friends in the acting profession and, as always, most of these seemed to be actresses. In fact, many of them were rather intimately involved with the writing of *Heartbreak House.*

According to Stanley Weintraub in *Journey to Heartbreak,* his book-long account of the composition of that play, its genesis was a story told to Shaw by Lena Ashwell. This very capable actress created the part of Lina Szczepanowska, the Polish acrobat, in Shaw's *Misalliance* in 1911, and they remained fast friends for many years. Shaw was looking for a protagonist for what was to become*Heart-break House* and was greatly intrigued when Miss Ashwell told him that her father had once been refused the last rites of the church because he insisted on having cheese with his communion wafer. Before taking holy orders in the Anglican Church, her father had lived a storybook life. At eleven he was a midshipman, and his first sea adventure was the capture of a slaveship, an experience which he had recounted to his daughter as he lay dying. This is why Shaw always referred to him as "a captain of souls." Not only that, but Miss Ashwell's early years were lived on a ship in the captain's quarters, complete with drawingroom and flower-filled terrace. This gave Shaw not only his protagonist Captain Shotover, but also the setting for this play, which is a country house built to resemble a Captain's quarters on a ship.

Miss Ashwell told him this story in 1913 and, as Shaw at one time observed, sometimes a character one hears about insists on being dramatized. He even used *Lena's Father* as the title for some time, although there were several working titles before the play was completed almost four years later.

One of the reasons Shaw took his time in writing this play was that he realized that, although the word "war" is never mentioned in the play, it is actually a war play. As he says in the preface, it is his version of Chekov's *The Cherry Orchard*, since it is cultured and leisured Europe (or England) drifting towards a war because of aimless frivolity. For this reason he had no intention of producing the play immediately since the only viable plays in the English theatre during the war were light comedies intended to entertain a war-weary nation.

By 1916, however, both Mrs. Pat Campbell and Lillah McCarthy had heard of the play by word-of-mouth and both wanted to produce it. Both of them wanted to play the part of the ingenue Ellie Dunn, though neither of them were in any way suited for it. Although actually central to the play, Shaw had inserted the role to suit the talents of Ellen O'Malley, who had created many of Shaw's heroines at the Court Theatre.

It was particularly hard for Shaw to refuse Lillah McCarthy permission to produce *Heartbreak House*. She was convinced that Ellie Dunn was the part she needed to revive her theatrical career, which had been in eclipse since her divorce from Granville Barker. "I am not deserting you, I am only facing the facts," Shaw explained to her. "The theatre just now is impossible. You should revive *Black-eyed Susan*. If [Henry] Ainley can dance a hornpipe well enough to produce the proper pattern . . . it would delight the Tommies and ruin the carpets with their tears." Shaw tried to make amends for this by writing her a short play, *Annajanska, The Wild Grand Duchess*, which he directed for her in person for a variety bill at the Coliseum.

After what Mrs. Pat Campbell had done to *Pygmalion*, it is small wonder that he refused to let her attempt the part of Ellie Dunn, although when the play was finally produced in 1921 at the Royal Court, it is surprising that he did not ask her to play the part of the forty-year-old siren, Hesione Hushabye. He had Mrs. Pat in mind constantly for Hesione as he wrote the play and she might have been what was needed to make it a success. It was, however, a failure.

Shaw was very disappointed and even went to the unprecedented length of asking the critics to come back a second time to see a slightly revised production. The reviews were still unfavorable and only sixty-three performances were given. Lillah McCarthy was right when she said that the play did not resemble Chekov's *Cherry Orchard* as much as it did Shakespeare's *Lear*. The critics, perhaps, were expecting another Shavian knock-about farce rather than Shaw's most serious play up to that time with overtones of tragedy, if not for the characters on the stage at least for the world in which they lived.

The Birmingham Repertory and the Theatre Guild

One of the most important professional associations of Shaw's later years was Barry Jackson, later to be knighted, who had founded the Birmingham Repertory Theatre in 1913 and who for twenty-two years maintained this creative playhouse in the face of great difficulties. Originally an

architect, he had decided to produce plays of artistic merit
rather than plays which might be successful financially.
Shortly after Shaw had written *Back to Methuselah* he
happened to turn up in Birmingham and attended a performance at the Birmingham Repertory Theatre. Sir Barry
presented himself to Shaw after the performance and asked
if he might produce *Methuselah*, which Shaw regarded as
his masterpiece in spite of its length. Shaw was a little skep-
tical and asked him how much a year he was out of pocket
from this cultural adventure in theatre management. Sir
Barry named an annual sum that would have been sufficient to support fifty laborers and their families. An agreement was therefore reached, and *Back to Methuselah* had
its English première at the Birmingham Repertory in October, 1923, the five plays being presented on five con-
secutive nights for four weeks. In February of the following
year the same company, with a few minor cast changes,
presented the play in the same manner at the Royal Court
in London. Thus Shaw found himself a patron and later
almost a partner in the production of many of his plays in
England during the waning years of his life.

In an introduction to *The Theatrical Companion to the
Plays of Shaw*, Sir Barry Jackson records that he subsequently discovered that Shaw was deeply grateful for the
fact that Jackson had in part made up for the bitter blow he
had received when Granville Barker had withdrawn from
the English theatre. Shaw had once again found a partner
for a second alliance in the theatre who was perhaps not as
brilliant or as versatile as Granville Barker had been, but
who produced his plays satisfactorily. Sir Barry had
been able to maintain a fairly permanent company over a
considerable number of years and for this reason the ensemble acting was often of a very high calibre. Shaw was
grateful and even sometimes, Sir Barry tells us, Shaw
treated him almost as a son, once even telling him not to
worry, but "trust to father."

Oddly enough it was because of his interest in finding
producers for *Back to Methuselah* that about the same time
Shaw became allied with another producing
organization—The Theatre Guild of New York. Shaw's per-

mission for production of his plays was obtained largely through the services of Lawrence Langner, one of the founders of the Guild and a member of the editorial board for many years. Langner's first contact with Shaw was actually made in 1911 when he was working as an apprentice in the office of Cruickshank & Fairweather, a Scottish firm of chartered patent agents in London. One of his employers, Wallace Cranston Fairweather, was a member of the Fabian Society and gave him a ticket to a Shaw lecture with the intriguing title, "The Position of the Artist Under Socialism." The lecture made a profound impression on the young man.

Shortly after this Langner emigrated to America and during the next two years became active with a group of young people living in Greenwich Village who were interested in the avant-garde drama of the day. The group included Walter Lippman, Philip Moeller, Waldo Frank, Kenneth McGowan, and Theresa Helburn. Members of the group would take part in play readings and at one of these Mr. Langner played opposite Miss Helburn in a reading of Shaw's playlet *Press Cuttings*. This, he tells us, was his only appearance in a Shaw play, but it led to a lifelong relationship with Miss Helburn. She became the director of The Washington Square Players, which organization in 1918 became The Theatre Guild.

One of the most ambitious projects of this group was to produce Shaw's *Mrs. Warren's Profession* at the Comedy Theatre in New York on March 11, 1918. At the first performance of this play in America at the Garrick Theatre in 1905 the actors had been arrested by the police and the play closed. Attitudes toward the treatment of the problem of prostitution in society had so changed by 1918 that the production not only did not interest the police but also failed to interest a large audience. The play survived for only 40 performances and paid neither Shaw his royalties, nor the landlord, Lee Shubert, the theatre rent.

In spite of this unpromising beginning, the fortunes of the Theatre Guild were made by the world première on November 10, 1920, of *Heartbreak House*. The play had greatly interested The Guild when it was published in 1919, and they immediately cabled for permission to produce it. Shaw wired his friend St. John Ervine, then in New York as a drama critic, for information about them. Since one of Guild's first successes was Ervine's play *John Ferguson,* he could assure him that the Guild was a reputable group, and Shaw forwarded a contract and specifications for the kind of scenery he wished the play to have.

What really endeared the Guild to Shaw was the fact that they became interested in a production of *Back to Methuselah,* and his advice to the Guild was much the same as it had been to Barry Jackson. When Langner asked for a contract, he told him that a contract was unnecessary since nobody but a lunatic would wish to produce it. This gave Langner his title *GBS and The Lunatic* for his history of Shaw's relationship with The Guild.

Ironically, Shaw never saw any of these Guild productions because, although many of them toured the United States, none were ever brought to London. Shaw himself was never in New York save for a three-day visit in 1933 when most of his time was engaged with a lecture at the Metropolitan Opera House for the American Association of Political Scientists. Some of the members of the Guild Board did see him briefly on board the cruise ship which was in the New York harbor. This did not mean that Shaw did not eventually get to know all of the Board members and many of the Guild performers, since all of them made pilgrimages to Number 10 Adelphi Terrace as well as Ayot St. Lawrence. He even saw Lynn Fontanne and Alfred Lunt in a London production of Sil-Vara's *Caprice,* and therefore had some idea of what this great acting team were able to do in his *Pygmalion, Arms and the Man,* and *Doctor's Dilemma.*

It could be safely said, however, that whatever the success of the Guild productions were, Shaw himself could not be as closely concerned with the details of production as he had been with Granville Barker at the Court Theatre or with Sir Barry Jackson at the Malvern Festival. On the other hand, the fact that many of Shaw's directives were transmitted by letter and cable meant that there is a fairly complete record of this preserved in the memoirs of the Guild directors, particularly those of Lawrence Langner.

In the last thirty years of his life the Guild produced sixteen Shaw plays in New York; six of these were world premières; and ten more Shaw plays were produced at the Westport Connecticut Playhouse which was used by the Guild for experimental productions in the summer. This total exceeds that of any other management in the history of Shaw's life in the theatre. In his dealings with the Guild, however, he is revealed more as a businessman, with a shrewd knowledge of what would play successfully, than as an artist and director.

Shaw at Malvern and the Old Vic

Shaw did not write another important play after *St. Joan* was finished in 1923 until *The Apple Cart* in 1929. At that time Sir Barry Jackson had decided to found the Malvern Festival in the little town which had been famous as a Victorian spa for many years. The first season was dedicated to Shaw, and the first year's program was devoted to his works entirely. Besides *The Apple Cart*, which had been especially written for the Festival, Sir Barry added a revival of *Back to Methuselah*, as well as productions of *Caesar and Cleopatra* and *Heartbreak House*. The company that performed these for several years thereafter was basically the Birmingham Repertory Company, although as the fame of the Festival grew, distinguished players were many times engaged for special parts. And now Shaw had his own festival that did honor to his genius, and for it the playwright, now in his seventies, wrote seven new plays.

Of these two, *The Apple Cart* (1929) and *In Good King Charles' Golden Days* (1939) are vintage Shaw. Perhaps Shaw was at his best writing about kings; and both of them basically were about the problems of finding suitable leaders—potential artist philosophers to guide England's destiny. Many of the other plays were dealt with harshly by some critics, but all of them contained some good Shaw; and all of them might be the envy of beginning playwrights.

The Malvern Theatre's auditorium space was excellent: 900 spectators could be comfortably seated. Also it adjoined the pump room and gardens where patrons

could stroll during intermission and where refreshments
were served. Backstage, however, the theatre was less than
adequate. There was little room for either scenery or
players and although this area was partly remodeled, it still
made plays with large casts and complicated scenery impossible. A new theatre was designed but the World War II
prevented its construction.

Shaw began the rehearsal procedure for Malvern in
much the same fashion as he had all other rehearsals of his
plays, with a reading of the play to the entire company.
"We started our rehearsals at the Old Vic in London,"
Cedric Hardwicke later recalled. "Shaw, tall and lean,
strode on to the bare stage, looking half like God and half
like a very malicious satyr. He sat down at a table in the
centre of the stage and began to read the play in his soft
Irish voice, every syllable clearly enunciated. That was
what he demanded from his actors and we got the full force
of his wrath and scorn if our pronunciation ever fell short of
that standard. 'You make Life Force sound like Live Horse'
he would say. He went further than just that. He used the
inflexions of his voice to differentiate each character. It was
an astonishing performance."[33]

Both Mr. and Mrs. Shaw looked forward to the annual
pilgrimage to Malvern for the Festival. Although Shaw did
not ever attempt to direct any of the seven new plays
himself from start to finish, he nearly always turned up at
some rehearsals. The director of the Festival, Mr. Roy
Limbert, recalls in particular a rehearsal he directed of a
revival of *You Never Can Tell* in 1934. The rehearsals
started at 11:00 since Shaw at seventy-eight said he was far
too old to have a long rehearsal. At 1:45 an exhausted actor
murmured something about lunch. Shaw apologized
profusely saying: "We'll go immediately to lunch." The
company breathed relief. "And," said GBS, "we'll be back
at 2:15 sharp." Back they were at 2:15 and continued until
5:00 when Limbert became a little worried. There was
another play to be given that night and a dress rehearsal
was needed. He gently drew Shaw's attention to the time
and Shaw was again apologetic.

On this occasion Shaw was directing a play which he

had directed many times before and Mr. Limbert described in detail how after each scene he would go up on the stage and act out all the parts for the company. One wonders if he remembered his first attempt to explain *You Never Can Tell* to Cyril Maude's Company at the Haymarket when no one understood what the play was about and it had to be withdrawn; or again the many revivals of the play under the Vedrenne-Barker Management when it was often the big money-maker that would make up for the losses incurred by less popular plays.

One of the difficulties at Malvern was the scarcity of rehearsals—only six for Wendy Hiller the summer she was recreating the difficult role of Eliza Doolittle and the same number for her performance of St. Joan. A letter to Miss Hiller is one of the last detailed analyses of the failure of an actress in the part. Shaw criticizes her for having done too much homework for her role, including the reading of his own preface to the play. In the preface he had defined Joan as a mystic and "Galtonic visualizer" who sincerely believed in her voices:

> What you have conceived is a cataleptic Joan, who in her highest moments goes out of the world into a trance. Such an effect is not impossible on the stage if the author has prepared it properly. If the play began with Joan in the fields with her sheep, hearing the bells, and going into a trance of ecstasy ending in a sleep from which she would be awakened by village folk who would discuss this strange power of hers so that the audience would learn about the trances and be able to recognize their symptoms, then you might produce an electric effect by making such a trance the climax of the cathedral scene and of the trial scene too, to say nothing of the epilogue.[34]

However, there was no scene in the play clearly dramatizing this. Rather Shaw had made his Joan a vigorous and forthright young woman, cutting through the pretensions of the hierarchy of church and state and at no time pausing in the midst of this to go into a trance. Miss Hiller's performance, therefore, was worse than disappointing, he said, it was infuriating and puzzling:

However, it is a bit of experience for you. One gets
experience by making mistakes. In future, when you want to
put something into your part that is not in the play, you
must ask the author—or some other author—to lead up to
the interpolation for you. Never forget that the effect of a
line may depend, not on its delivery but on something said
earlier in the play either by somebody else or by yourself,
and that if you change it, it may be necessary to change the
whole first act as well. Now I can't rewrite *Joan* for you,
though it would be great fun.—G.B.S.[35]

Whether Miss Hiller was able to incorporate this advice into the few remaining performances of the play at
Malvern is doubtful. Shaw, however, is here again revealed
as a kind but discerning critic of acting. On the whole he
approved of Miss Hiller's Joan and wanted her to play the
part in the movie version of the play which Gabriel Pascal
was contemplating doing as the war broke out. Having
created two of Shaw's greatest heroines for the
screen—Eliza and Barbara—it is a great loss that Miss
Hiller was never able to add Joan to her list of triumphs.

What distinguishes the Malvern productions of his
plays from the earlier ones is that he had much more control
over them; he had worked with many members of the cast
before and knew what kind of a performance he could get
from them. The born teacher had discovered a few short
cuts in teaching the players how to recognize the "tunes" in
his plays. In helping them with revivals he knew where the
pitfalls were—and there are pitfalls even in the greatest
plays.

Shaw probably died thinking that his Festival at
Malvern would continue after his death. He had seen and
approved of the plans for the new theatre, a part of which
had already been built, and by this time he had, like his
Captain Shotover, reached the "seventh level of concen-
tration," and the fame and the glory of the material world
mattered little. He had even made his peace with his rival
Shakespeare in a puppet play written for the Festival entitled *Shakes versus Shav*. He said in the preface:

'This in all actuarial probability is my last play and the
climax of my eminence, such as it is. I thought my career as

a playwright was finished when Waldo Lanchester of the Malvern Marionette Theatre, our chief living puppet master, sent me figures of two puppets, Shakespeare and myself, with a request that I should supply one of my famous dramas for them.[36]

Shaw always had a weakness for puppet plays as well as for knock-about farce, hence he evolved a short play in which "Shakes" attacks the upstart "Shav" as a rival. Shakes knocks Shav down for a count of nine and then is himself knocked down. Shakes asks Shav if he could have written *King Lear;* and Shav challenges Shakes to have written *Heartbreak House,* but, almost humbly since both are mortal, he asks the bard to let for a moment his "glimmering light to shine."

Shaw in his program note maintains that he learned his craft as a director from puppets. Like Gordon Craig, he felt that they were in some respects superior to living actors since the unvarying intensity of facial expression, which is impossible for living actors, keeps the imagination of the audience continuously stimulated. Shaw had to write many nasty notes to young actors who wanted to "react" to every line of every speech of the other players. Unless specifically told by the director (or Shaw himself) to begin reacting, they were to be as motionless as statues. Ellen Pollock, who created Sweetie for Shaw's *Too True to be Good* in 1934 and went on to play in more Shaw revivals than any other actress, has in her possession an unpublished letter about this very matter. She was to appear as Major Barbara and was concerned (as other actresses have been) about the long scene in the last act in which her father, Sir Andrew Undershaft, and her fiance discuss the future of "the factory of death" without her having a single line. Shaw's specific instructions were that she was simply to listen intently since her whole future depends on their decision, but not to move as much as an eyelash.

Miss Pollock's playing of Sweetie in the London production of *Too True to be Good* launched her on a long career as actress on stage, screen, and television. Many other players could say the same. Sir Cedric Hardwicke in his biography *A Victorian in Orbit* admits that it was as an

actor in Shaw plays at Birmingham and Malvern that made
him a star. He had profited from the many postcards and
notes, one of which accuses him of giving his big speech in
The Apple Cart without pronouncing a single conjunction
or preposition! Edith Evans, Eileen Beldon, Gwen
Ffrongcon-Gavis, Scott Sunderland, Cecil Trouncer—all
were provincial nobodies who achieved distinction and
sometimes stardom because of their work in Shaw's plays at
Malvern.

At the Malvern Festival Shaw did as he had been doing
more and more frequently since the dissolution of the
Shaw-Barker team. After the initial reading of the play to
the cast, most of the blocking of the play in the all too few
rehearsals was turned over to Sir Barry Jackson's veteran
cadre which he had brought with him from Birmingham
and which included H. K. Ayliff, Herbert Prentis, Paul
Sheveling, Marion Spencer, and others. Of course he could
not resist the notes and letters to the cast and in the thirteen
Shaw revivals he often sprang into action with a vigor unbelievable for a man who, at the last Festivals before the
war, was in his eighties.

Shaw's fame as a playwright was now firmly established and many other managements in England were
organized with repertories in which his plays were always a
part. For instance, in 1924 Charles Macdona engaged Esme
Percy to direct and play in some Shaw plays, including the
long neglected *Mrs. Warren's Profession,* and the Macdona
Players appeared in English cities that had never heard of
Shaw. Similarly, Lilian Baylis did eleven Shaw revivals at
the Old Vic, after her productions of Shakespeare with John
Gielgud, Ralph Richardson, and Lawrence Olivier had
begun attracting West End Theatre goers across the
Thames and down Waterloo Road to the dingy old theatre
that was shortly to become famous.

Ralph Richardson recalls Shaw coming to the rehearsals of *Arms and the Man,* under the direction of his old
friend Harcourt Williams, at the Old Vic. Shaw found
Richardson having a great deal of trouble with the first act
of the play. Bluntchli, having escaped from his enemy,
climbs up a drainpipe and in through a window in a terrific

state of exhaustion. Richardson knew that he must get this utter exhaustion into his characterization but was having difficulty. Shaw came to him and said:

> You know, Richardson, I'd like to have a word with you about your Bluntchli. It's going to be a very fine Bluntchli I am sure . . . but you know there's one thing the matter with your Bluntchli. When you come in, you show that you're very upset, you spend a long time with your gasps and your pauses and your lack of breath and your dizziness and your tiredness. It's very well done, it's very well done indeed, but it doesn't suit my play. It's no good for me, it's no good for Bernard Shaw. You've got to go from line to line, quickly and swiftly, never stop the flow of lines, never stop. It's one joke after another, it's a firecracker. Always reserve the acting for underneath the spoken word. It's a musical play, a knockabout musical comedy.[37]

Shaw's Legacy to the Players

During Shaw's last years, when he was not able to direct players on the stage itself, many came to him. Blanche Patch recalls arriving at Ayot St. Lawrence to find Gertrude Lawrence, about to begin work on *Pygmalion*, perched on the edge of Shaw's bed singing duets with him. Also Ellen Pollock, who not only played Eliza several times but also had directed *Pygmalion*, often visited the playwright whom she claims to have "adored almost to the point of adulation." One wonders whether as he coached these actresses if he recalled the voices of the other Elizas who had come to him for advice and encouragement.

Other distinguished players came to Ayot St. Lawrence. Greer Garson, who re-created several important Shaw roles was a frequent visitor. Maurice Evans brought with him most of the cast that was to join him in his revivals of *The Apple Cart* and *Man and Superman*. In 1949, the entire cast of the new Shaw play *Bouyant Billions* came to rehearse on the lawn.

Shaw's fifty years on stage offered a rare phenomenon—a dramatist-director at work. When Shaw said he was a very old-fashioned playwright he meant just that. And this also means that in one sense he was a very

old-fashioned director. At a time when the Moscow Art
Theatre was producing plays in which the director was
giving much of his attention to crowd scenes, Shaw was not
interested; there were few crowds in any of the plays he
wrote. He was interested only in the principals to whom he
gave great solos, duets, trios, and quartets; but he never
went beyond an occasional octette. Similarly, when players,
trained in the Stanislavsky method, began evolving complicated "sub-texts" for their performances, he immediately put a stop to it. Sir Cedric Hardwicke recalls that when
he was rehearsing *Caesar*, Shaw found him with a book on
Egyptology which he advised him to put aside. All that was
needed were Shaw's own words and stage directions. Even
his prefaces were for readers not actors.

Great acting on the stage is at best an ephemeral
thing. When the curtain goes down on the last performance of a production, all that really is left are the reviews
and interviews (frequently more revealing than the
reviews). To this may be added the biographies that great
actors may write. But Shaw gave the theatre something infinitely more balanced in his notes and letters, often written
by flashlight in the darkened auditorium as he watched his
actors rehearse.

If one were to isolate any one contribution to the art of
directing it would be his insistence on the training of actors
to catch the rhythm of the dialogue in play, to vary it and to
build the cadence of their big speeches from line to line.
When in 1921 a young American actress, Molly Tompkins,
came to Shaw for advice on how to perfect her craft, he admonished her as follows:

> . . . what you want is work, or rather sheer drudgery to put
> up your muscle, and give you the hard driven professional
> touch that comes from doing a thing every day for ten years
> and in no other way. Without that, although you may know
> how a thing should be done, and understand it a thousand
> times better than a hack fifty-dollar-a-week actress, she will
> "get it across" more effectively than you. I don't know
> whether you are a musician. If not, you don't know Mozart;
> and if you dont know Mozart you will never understand my
> technique. If you are, you must have noticed sometime or

another that though a composer may play his music ever so much more beautifully and intelligently than a professional pianist, yet he cannot produce the same effect in a concert room, because he hasn't got the steel in his fingers. You have to get steel in the muscles of your face, and steel in your heart, by hammering away every day (or night) until you can hit the boy at the back of the gallery in a three hundred pound house. Don't think that at present you can reach only three rows of stalls, and that as you go on you will carry a row further and yet another row until you get to the wall. That's not it at all. You can reach the boy all right now, just as you can reach the conductor of the band. But you can't take possession of him and hold him up above the discomfort of his cheap seat.[38]

The emphasis was from first to last on the spoken word, and what is sometimes called the "art of acting"—the long and "pregnant" pause—was contemptuously discarded. He could not tolerate the "eloquent silence," to use another critical cliche, any more than the conductor of an orchestra could arbitrarily hold a rest for longer than the score indicated.

Perhaps Shaw's greatest permanent influence on the art of acting in the English-speaking world was in the formation of the Royal Academy of Dramatic Art. Even while a dramatic critic in the nineties, he argued with those who felt that a school of acting in England was unnecessary since the stock companies in the provinces were really a school of acting. In his own column in the *Saturday Review* Shaw attacked this violently.

The stock actor, according to Shaw, quite simply developed for himself a number of tricks which he used over and over again:

The stock actor solved the problem by adopting a "line"; for example, if his "line" was old age, he acquired a trick of doddering and speaking in a cracked voice: if juvenility, he swaggered and effervesced. With these accomplishments, eked out by a few rules of thumb as to wigs and face-painting, one deplorable step dance, and one still more deplorable "combat," he "swallowed" every part given to him in a couple of hours, and regurgitated it in the evening

over the footlights, always in the same manner, however
finely the dramatist might have individualized it. His in-
famous incompetence at last swept him from the reputable
theatres into the barns and booths; and it was then that he
became canonized, in the imagination of a posterity that had
never suffered from him, as the incarnation of the one quality in which he was quite damnably deficient; to wit, ver-
satility. His great contribution to dramatic art was the knack
of earning a living for fifty years on the stage without ever
really acting, or either knowing or caring for the difference
between the Comedy of Errors and Box and Cox.[39]

Shaw was quite definite about what an acting school
should and should not be. He begins by refuting the
suggestion that what was needed was something like the
Conservatoire of the Comédie Française. This kind of an institution teaches that "there is one right way (all others are
wrong) of taking a chair and sitting down on it, or kneeling
at a lady's feet, or picking up a handkerchief, of howling an
alexandrine, and shaking hands." The result would be that
although it could train a housemaid to perform the Queen
in *Ruy Blas* without committing a single error, the performance would be so completely machine-made that it would
be but a hollow shell of a characterization. An actor, he continues, is by definition a person born with the faculty of acting, but that faculty is limited by the power of the actor to
execute his conceptions. He then summarizes what every
actor should have:

> He should first have a skilled command of his nerves and
> muscles for relaxation and inertion (*sic*) as well as stimula-
> tion and exertion . . . his organs of speech should be trained
> like a pianist's fingers, until he can strike a consonant as
> Paderewski strikes a note . . . he should especially have com-
> plete control of the muscles of his face. He should have an
> expert's ear for phonetics, and be able with promptitude and
> certainty to pronounce from 12 to 20 pure vowels, and com-
> bine them into dipthongs, practicing them with the alphabet
> every day as Madame Patti (*sic*) practices her scales and so
> acquiring the power to analyze dialectics and foreign
> sounds, and reproduce them scientifically instead of merely
> mimicing their most salient traits.[40]

These are, Shaw maintains, the true qualities required by the actor. Everything else is mere accomplishment that can be learned from a teacher.

But the greatest difficulty would be to find these teachers. The teaching of singing by people who have failed as singers is destructive and ruinous. "I am not proposing," says Shaw, "a fresh opening for the sort of gentleman who plays the Soothsayer for 50 shillings a week on the stage, and is ready off it to teach somebody how to play Brutus and Anthony for half a guinea a lesson." Again Shaw insists that acting should be a profession only for persons of great energy of character, indomitable industry, and unconquerable vocation. It should not be a place for dilettantes.

All this discussion of what the nature of a "histrionic school" should be was shortly to bring about tangible results. In 1904, just seven years later, the Royal Academy of Dramatic Arts was founded. Shaw immediately took an active interest and in 1911 was elected to the Council. Almost immediately he began campaigning to make it a public institution in which speech, deportment, and acting could be taught and for which eventually government recognition would be sought. Students of approved ability should receive a government subsidy for this and for the rest of their education. In 1921 this aim was somewhat realized when Royal patronage was conferred on the institution. Shaw was especially pleased when London County Council scholarships for dramatic art were obtained and when a diploma in dramatic art was recognized by the University of London.

Shaw was also instrumental in putting the Academy on the same footing with the public as the Royal College of Music. Music since 1843 had been recognized as a fine art. Shaw contributed five thousand pounds toward the erection of a new building in Gower Street. Today Shaw's bust stands in the foyer. He also anonymously contributed to a little volume called *The R.A.D.A. Graduates Keepsake and Counselor* in which he concluded with the sound advice to the new graduate that "his personal reputation and professional achievements are henceforth bound up with the creed, not only of the academy, but with that of the understanding of the theatrical art in the civilized world." Shaw himself was aware that neither a famous actor nor a famous author had a private life that is completely his own. A great deal of the reputation of the Royal Academy of Dramatic Art today is due not only to his interest, which began at the turn of the century, but to the fact that it is the recipient of something like one-third of the revenue from Shaw's estate, which makes it a very wealthy institution indeed.

In terms of his own playwriting Shaw always felt that it was his function to prophecy and interpret the next stage of creative evolution; the same might be said to be true of Shaw the director. He expected the actors in his plays to give him more than their best performances, and they heard from him if they didn't do so. The one message to them that comes through consistently is that they must be bigger than life-size. Their training of themselves for this task must be as rigorous and as dedicated as that of a great musician. Thus inspired, many of them gave such performances, and there is a magnificent record, much in Shaw's own words, of a great era in theatrical history.

Notes

CHAPTER I

1. Frances Donaldson, *The Actor-Managers* (London: Weidenfeld and Nicolson, 1970), p. 11.
2. William Archer, "A Preface to Theatrical World of 1893," *Shaw on Theatre*, ed. E. J. West (New York: Hill and Wang, 1959), p. 44.
3. *Ellen Terry and Bernard Shaw: A Correspondence*, ed. Christopher St. John (New York: G. P. Putnam's Sons, 1931), p. 135.
4. *Bernard Shaw Collected Letters 1874-1897*, ed. Dan H. Laurence (New York: Dodd, Mead and Company, 1965), p. 458.
5. *Ibid.*, p. 524.
6. Archibald Henderson, *George Bernard Shaw: Man of the Century* (New York: Appleton-Century-Crofts, Inc., 1956), p. 452n.
7. *Collected Letters*, p. 829.
8. *Ibid.*
9. *Shaw, Man of the Century*, p. 450
10. *Ibid.*, p. 451.
11. *Ibid.*, p. 511.
12. Lawrence Langner, *G.B.S. and the Lunatic* (New York: Atheneum Publishers, 1963), p. 12.
13. *Shaw, Man of the Century*, p. 477n.
14. *G.B.S. and the Lunatic*, p. 13.
15. "My Way with a Play," *Shaw on Theatre*, ed. E. J. West (New York: Hill and Wang, 1959), p. 269.
16. Jacques Barzun, "Bernard Shaw in Twilight," *George Bernard Shaw: A Critical Survey*, ed. Louis Kronenberger (New York and Cleveland: The World Publishing Company, 1953), p. 166.
17. Martin Meisel, *Shaw and the Nineteenth Century Theatre* (Princeton, N.J.: Princeton University Press, 1963), p. 121.
18. George Bernard Shaw, "Too True to be Good," *Complete Plays and Prefaces* (New York: Dodd, Mead and Company, 1962), 4:670.
19. Eric Bentley, *Bernard Shaw* (New York: New Directions Books, 1957), pp. xxii, xxiii.
20. Bernard Shaw, "Qualifications of the Complete Actor," *The*

Dramatic Review, summarized by Drew S. Pallette in *The Shaw Review*, 4, No. 1 (January 1961).

21. "Shaw on del Sartism" (reprinted from the "Art Corner" of *Our Corner*, September 1, 1886; *The Independent Shavian*, 5, No. 2, Fall 1966).

22. "Acting, by One Who Does Not Believe in It," (1889), reprinted in *Bernard Shaw: Platform and Pulpit*, ed. Dan H. Laurence (New York: Hill and Wang, 1961).

23. William Archer, *Masks or Faces*, introd. Lee Strasberg (New York: Hill and Wang, Inc., 1957).

24. *Shaw: Platform and Pulpit*, p. 22.

25. "The Play of Ideas," *Shaw on Theatre*, p. 294.

26. Charles Lloyd Holt, "Candida: the Music of Ideas," *The Shaw Review*, 9, No. 1 (January 1966), p. 2.

27. Theodore Stier, "Barker and Shaw at the Court Theatre, A View from the Pit." *The Shaw Review*, 10, No. 1 (January 1967), pp. 20-21.

28. "Sybil Thorndike with Michael Macowan," *Great Acting*, ed. Hal Burton (New York: Hill and Wang, 1967), p. 59.

29. *Ibid.*, p. 58.

30. *Ibid.*, p. 174.

31. *Ibid.*, p. 174.

CHAPTER II

1. Preface to "London Music 1888-1889," *Shaw on Music*, ed. Eric Bentley (Garden City: Doubleday and Company, Inc., 1955), p. 7.

2. R. F. Rattray, *Bernard Shaw: A Chronicle* (New York: Roy Publications, 1951), p. 14.

3. Archibald Henderson, *Bernard Shaw: Playboy and Prophet* (New York and London: D. Appleton and Company, 1932), pp. 46, 47.

4. Bernard Shaw, "Biographers Blunders Corrected," *Sixteen Self Sketches* (New York: Dodd, Mead and Company, 1949).

5. Bernard Shaw, *How to Become a Musical Critic*, previously uncollected writings, ed. Dan H. Laurence (New York: Hill and Wang, 1961), p. 219.

6. Corno Di Bassetto (Bernard Shaw), *London Music in 1888-1889* (London: Constable and Company, Ltd., 1937), p. 21.

7. Bernard Shaw, *Sixteen Self Sketches* (New York: Dodd, Mead and Company, 1949), p. 60.

8. *London Music in 1888-1889*, p. 29.

9. *Ibid.*, p. 17.

10. B. C. Rosset, *Shaw of Dublin* (University Park, Pa: Pennsylvania State University Press, 1964), p. 335.

11. Bernard Shaw, *Complete Plays with Prefaces* (New York: Dodd, Mead and Company, 1962), 1:192.

12. *Ibid.*, pp. 193-94.

13. *Ibid.*, p. 202.

14. *Ibid.*, p. 199.
15. St. John Greer Ervine, *Bernard Shaw: His Life, Work and Friends* (New York: William Morrow and Company, Inc., 1956), p. 281.
16. John A. Mills, "The Comic in Words: Shaw's Cockney," *Drama Survey*, 1, No. 2 (Summer 1966), p. 139.
17. *Complete Plays* 1:692.
18. *Ibid.*, p. 206.

CHAPTER III

1. *An Unfinished Novel by Bernard Shaw*, ed. with Introd. Stanley Weintraub (London: Constable, 1958), p. 8.
2. Bernard Shaw, *Love Among the Artists* (New York: Brentano's, 1927), p. 300.
3. *Collected Letters*, p. 188.
4. *Florence Farr, Bernard Shaw, W. B. Yeats: Letters*, ed. Clifford Bax (London: Home and Van Thal, Ltd., 1946), p. 6.
5. *Ibid.*, p. 1.
6. *Ibid.*, p. 2.
7. *Shaw on Theatre*, p. 5.
8. *Farr, Shaw, Yeats: Letters*, pp. 5, 6.
9. *Ibid.*, pp. 6, 7.
10. *Ibid.*, p. 9.
11. Raymond Mander and Joe Mitchenson, *The Theatrical Companion to the Plays of Shaw* (New York: Pitman Publishing Company, 1955), p. 37.
12. *Farr, Shaw, Yeats: Letters*, pp. 10-11.
13. *Ibid.*, p. 12.
14. *Collected Letters*, p. 492.
15. *Ibid.*, p. 337.
16. *Ibid.*, p. 338.
17. *Ibid.*, pp. 492-93.

CHAPTER IV

1. *Collected Letters*, p. 379.
2. *Ibid.*, p. 380.
3. *Ibid.*, p. 382.
4. *Ibid.*, pp. 385-86.
5. Bernard Shaw, *Dramatic Opinions and Essays with an Apology by Bernard Shaw* (New York: Brentano's, 1906), 2: 114.
6. *Ibid.*, p. 112.
7. *Ibid.*, p. 116.
8. *Ibid.*, pp. 124-25.
9. *Ellen Terry and Bernard Shaw: A Correspondence*, p. 103.
10. *Dramatic Opinions and Essays*, 2: 214-15.
11. *Shaw's Dramatic Criticism from The Saturday Review*, ed. Hohn F. Matthews (New York: Hill and Wang, 1959), p. 233.

12. *Ibid.*, p. 234.
13. "On Being a Lady in High Comedy," *Shaw on Theatre*, p. 81.
14. "Granville-Barker: Some Particulars," *Shaw on Theatre*, p. 260.
15. C. B. Purdom, *Harley Granville Barker* (London: Barrie & Rockcliff, 1955), p. 20.
16. St. John Ervine, p. 34.
17. Purdom, *Harley Granville Barker*, p. 15.
18. *Shaw on Theatre*, p. 106.
19. *Ibid.*, p. 107.
20. *Ibid.*, p. 108.
21. *Ibid.*, p. 109.
22. *Shaw on Theatre*, p. 281.
23. Henderson, *Man of the Century*, p. 670.
24. Lillah McCarthy, O.B.E., *Myself and My Friends, with an aside by Bernard Shaw* (New York: Dutton and Co., 1933), p. 5
25. Purdom, *Harley Granville Barker*, p. 60.
26. Bentley, pp. 225-27.
27. C. B. Purdom, *Bernard Shaw's Letters to Granville Barker*, with commentary and notes (New York: Theatre Arts Books, 1957), p. 173.
28. Brooks Atkinson, "Everybody Was in Love With Ellen," *New York Times Book Review*, May 26, 1968, p. 24.
29. *Terry and Shaw: A Correspondence*, pp. 240-41.
30. *Ibid.*, p. 246.
31. *Ibid.*, p. 303.
32. Purdom, *Bernard Shaw's Letters to Granville Barker*, p. 58.
33. Purdom, *Harley Granville Barker*, p. 55.
34. Bentley, pp. 223-24.
35. Purdom, *Harley Granville Barker*, p. 70.
36. *Ibid.*, p. 106.
37. *Ibid.*, p. 124.
38. Hesketh Pearson, *G.B.S. A Full Length Portrait* (New York and London: Harper and Brothers, 1942), p. 258.
39. Purdom, *Harley Granville Barker*, p. 139.

CHAPTER V

1. Mrs. Pat Campbell, *My Life and Some Letters* (New York and London: Benjamin Blom, 1922), p. 273.
2. *Terry and Shaw: A Correspondence*, p. 186.
3. *Ibid.*, pp. 326-27
4. *Ibid.*, p. 328.
5. *Bernard Shaw and Mrs. Patrick Campbell: Their Correspondence*, ed. Alan Dent (New York: Alfred A. Knopf, 1952), p. 14.
6. *Ibid.*, p. 16.
7. *Ibid.*, pp. 18-19.
8. St. John Ervine, p. 446.
9. *Shaw and Campbell: Their Correspondence*, p. 152.

10. *Ibid.*, p. 153.
11. *Ibid.*, pp. 154-55.
12. *Ibid.*, p. 166.
13. *Ibid.*, pp. 180-81.
14. *Ibid.*, p. 181.
15. *Complete Plays*, 1: 245.
16. *Theatrical Companion*, p. 160.
17. *Shaw and Campbell: Their Correspondence*, p. 229.
18. *Ibid.* pp. 238-39.
19. *Ibid.*, pp. 379-80.
20. *Ibid.*, pp. 381-82.
21. *Ibid.*, p. 332.
22. Jesse Torn, "A Figleaf in Her Bonnet: A Scene and a Preface," *The . Shaw Review*, 5, No. 2, May 1962, p. 61
23. *Ibid.*, p. 62.
24. Purdom, *Harley Granville Barker*, p. 170.
25. *Ibid.*, pp. 174-75.
26. *Ibid.*, p. 279.
27. *Shaw's Letters to Granville Barker*, pp. 199-200.
28. *Ibid.*, p. 53.
29. *Ibid.*, p. 99.
30. *Shaw's Letters to Granville Barker*, pp. 105-6.
31. Purdom, *Harley Granville Barker*, p. 22.
32. St. John Ervine, pp. 343-44.
33. R. S. Minney, *Recollections of Bernard Shaw* (Englewood Cliffs: Prentice Hall, 1969), pp. 114-15.
34. *Ibid.*, p. 117.
35. *Ibid.*, pp. 117-18.
36. *Theatrical Companion*, p. 272.
37. *Great Acting*, p. 68.
38. *To a Young Actress: The Letters of Bernard Shaw to Molly Tompkins*, ed. with introd. by Peter Tompkins (New York: Clarkston H. Potter, 1960), pp. 11-12.
39. *The /London/ Morning Post*, reprinted in *The Shaw Review*, 11, No. 2, May 1968, p. 52.
40. *Ibid.*, p. 62.

Bibliography

WORKS BY SHAW

Advice to a Young Critic. Edited by E. J. West. New York: Crown Publishers, 1955.

Bernard Shaw and Mrs. Patrick Campbell: Their Correspondence. Edited by Alan Dent. New York: Alfred A. Knopf, 1952.

Bernard Shaw's Letters to Granville Barker. Edited by C. B. Purdom. New York: Theatre Arts Books, 1957.

Collected Letters, 1874-1897. Edited by Dan H. Laurence. New York: Dodd, Mead and Company, 1965.

Collected Letters, 1898-1910. Edited by Dan H. Laurence. New York: Dodd, Mead and Company, 1972.

Complete Plays with Prefaces. 6 vols. New York: Dodd, Mead and Company, 1962.

Dramatic Opinions and Essays with an Apology by Bernard Shaw. 2 vols. New York: Bretano's, 1906.

Ellen Terry and Bernard Shaw: A Correspondence. Edited by Christopher St. John. New York: G. P. Putnam's Sons, 1931.

Florence Farr, Bernard Shaw, W. B. Yeats: Letters. Edited by Clifford Bax. London: Home and Van Thal, Ltd., 1946.

How to Become a Musical Critic. Edited by Dan H. Laurence. New York: Hill and Wang, 1961.

London Music in 1888-1889. London: Constable and Company, Ltd. 1937.

Love Among the Artists. London: Constable and Company, 1950.

Major Critical Essays. London: Constable and Company, 1955.

Music in London, 1890-94. 3 vols. London: Constable and Company, 1956.

Our Theatres in the Nineties. 3 vols. London: Constable and Company, 1948.

Pen Portraits and Reviews. London: Constable and Company, 1949.

Platform and Pulpit. Edited by Dan H. Laurence, New York: Hill and Wang, 1961.

Prefaces by Bernard Shaw. London: Odhams Press Ltd., 1938.

161

"The Religion of the Pianoforte." *Fortnightly Review*, LV (n.s.): 254-66.

Religious Speeches of Bernard Shaw. Edited by Warren S. Smith. University Park: Pennsylvania State University Press, 1963.

Shaw on Shakespeare. Edited by Edwin Wilson. New York: E. P. Dutton and Company, Inc., 1961.

Shaw on Theatre. Edited by E. J. West. New York: Hill and Wang, 1959.

Sixteen Self-Sketches. New York: Dodd, Mead and Company, 1949.

Table Talk of G.B.S. New York and London: Harper and Brothers, 1925.

To a Young Actress. Edited by Peter Tomkins. New York: Clarkson N. Potter, 1960.

OTHER WORKS

Agate, James, ed. *The English Dramatic Critics*. New York: Hill and Wang, n.d. [1960?].

Bentley, Eric. *Bernard Shaw*. New York: New Directions Books, 1957.

————. *The Playwright as Thinker*. New York: Reynal and Hitchcock, 1946.

Chesterton, G. K. *George Bernard Shaw*. New York: Hill and Wang, 1956.

Crompton, Louis. *Shaw the Dramatist*. Lincoln: University of Nebraska Press, 1969.

Donaldson, Frances. *The Actor-Managers*. London: Weidenfeld and Nicolson, 1970.

Du Cann, G. C. L. *The Loves of G.B.S.* New York: Funk and Wagnalls Co., Inc., 1963.

Dunbar, Janet. *Mrs. G.B.S.* London: George C. Harrap and Co., Ltd., 1963.

Ervine, St. John Greer. *Bernard Shaw: His Life, Work and Friends*. New York: William Morrow and Company, Inc., 1956.

Franc, Miriam A. *Ibsen in England*. Boston: The Four Seas Company, 1919.

Gassner, John. "Shaw on Ibsen and the Drama of Ideas." *Ideas in the Drama* (7). New York and London: Columbia University Press, 1964, pp. 71-100.

Gerould, Daniel Charles. "George Bernard Shaw's Criticism of Ibsen." *Comparative Literature*, XV, no. 1: 130-45.

Glicksberg, C. O. "The Criticism of Bernard Shaw." *South Atlantic Quarterly*, L: 96-108.

Hankin, St. J. "Bernard Shaw as a Critic." *Fortnightly Review*, LXXXVII: 1057-68.

Harris, Frank. *Bernard Shaw*. New York: Simon and Schuster, 1931.

Henderson, Archibald. *George Bernard Shaw: Man of the Century*. New York: Appleton-Century-Crofts, Inc., 1956.

————. *Bernard Shaw: Playboy and Prophet*. New York and London: D. Appleton and Company, 1932.

Irvine, William. *The Universe of G.B.S.* New York: Whittlesey House, McGraw-Hill, 1949.

Joad, C. E. M. *Shaw.* London: Victor Gollancz Ltd., 1949.

Kaufmann, R. J. ed. *G. B. Shaw: A Collection of Critical Essays.* Englewood Cliffs, N.J.: Prentice-Hall, Inc., 1965.

Kaye, Julian B. *Bernard Shaw and the Nineteenth-Century Tradition.* Norman: University of Oklahoma Press, 1959.

Kronenberger, Louis, ed. *George Bernard Shaw: A Critical Survey.* New York and Cleveland: The World Publishing Co., 1953.

Langner, Lawrence. *G.B.S. and the Lunatic.* New York: Atheneum Publishers, 1963.

Mander, Raymond, and Mitchenson, Joe, *The Theatrical Companion to the Plays of Shaw.* New York: Pitman Publishing Company, 1955.

Meisel, Martin. *Shaw and the Nineteenth Century Theatre.* Princeton, N.J.: Princeton University Press, 1963.

Mills, John A. *Language and Laughter: Comic Diction in the Plays of Bernard Shaw.* Tucson: University of Arizona Press, 1969.

Nethercot, Arthur H. *The First Five Lives of Annie Besant.* Chicago: University of Chicago Press, 1960.

––––––. *Men and Supermen: The Shavian Portrait Gallery.* Cambridge: Harvard University Press, 1954.

Nicoll, Allardyce. *A History of Late Nineteenth Century Drama: 1850-1900.* 2 vols. Cambridge: Cambridge University Press, 1959.

Ohmann, Richard. *Shaw: The Style and the Man.* Middletown, Conn.: Wesleyan University Press, 1962.

Orme, Michael (Mrs. Alice Augusta Grein). *J. T. Grein: The Story of a Pioneer.* London: J. D. Muray, 1936.

Pearson, Hesketh. *G.B.S. A Full Length Portrait.* New York and London: Harper and Brothers, 1942.

––––––. *G.B.S. A Postscript.* New York: Harper and Brothers, 1950.

Rattray, R. F. *Bernard Shaw: A Chronicle.* New York: Roy Publications, 1951.

Rossett, Benjamin C. *Shaw of Dublin, The Formative Years.* University Park: Pennsylvania State University Press, 1964.

Rowell, George. *The Victorian Theatre.* London: Oxford University Press, 1956.

Silverman, Albert H. "Bernard Shaw's Shakespeare Criticism." *PMLA,* LXXII: 722-36.

Smith, J. P. "Superman vs. Man: Bernard Shaw on Shakespeare," *Yale Review,* XLII: 75-76.

Smith, Percy J. *The Unrepentant Pilgrim. A Study of the Development of Bernard Shaw.* Boston: Houghton Mifflin Co., 1965.

Smith, Robert McCaughan. "Modern Dramatic Censorship: George Bernard Shaw." Ph.D. dissertation, Indiana University, 1953.

Speaight, Robert. *William Poel and the Elizabethan Revival.* London: William Heinemann Ltd., 1954.

Ward, A. C. *Bernard Shaw.* New York: Longmans, Green, 1952.

West, E. J. "G.B.S., Music and Shakespearean Blank Verse." *University of Colorado Studies*, Series B. (Humanities), II: 344-56.

Williamson, Audrey. *Bernard Shaw: Man and Writer*. New York: Crowell-Collier Press, 1963.

Wilson, Colin. *Bernard Shaw: A Reassessment*. New York: Atheneum Publishers, 1969.

Winsten, Stephen. *G.B.S. at 90*. New York: Dodd, Mead and Co., 1946.

Index